I
AM
WHAT
I
DO

Contemplation
and
Human Experience

I
AM
WHAT
I
DO

Contemplation
and
Human Experience

by
Barbara Doherty

THE THOMAS MORE PRESS
Chicago, Illinois

ISBN 0-88347-129-9

Contents

FOR MARGARET: A CONTEMPLATIVE

ACKNOWLEDGMENTS

Five women in particular surrounded the beginnings of this book with love and community: Jody, Judy, Barbara, Jean and Celeste; all sisters of Providence.

Gratitude to the readers who supported me with helpful comments: Nancy Nolan, S.P., Theresa M. Takacs, S.P., Denise Wilkinson, S.P., Charles Fisher, priest of the Archdiocese of Indianapolis, and Paul Walsh, FSC.

Lastly, thanks to those who typed and edited: Ann O'Connor, S.P., and Elizabeth Clare Vrabely, S.P.

CHAPTER ONE

Religious Experience

Go up on a high mountain, joyful messenger to Zion. Shout
with a loud voice, joyful messenger to Jerusalem. Shout without fear, say to the town of Judah, "Here is your God." Here
is the Lord Yahweh coming with power, his arm subduing all
things to him. The prize of his victory is with him, his trophies
all go before him.

Is. 40/9-10

THE people we read about in the scriptures seem so
easily able to perceive God acting in their midst; in contrast, we drag our feet from day to day wishing some
sign of God's presence would erupt in the ever-so-daily
sense we have of our lives. The presumption we make is
that the Israelites saw great miracles worked in their
midst and that they had great religious experiences
while we really never feel God's manifestation. Someone needs to tell us that our presumption is erroneous;
our God does act now in the same way that God acted in
all of history but we read our scriptures too superfi-
cially.

In the passage quoted above we find the thoughts of a
man who was in exile in Babylon for many years; we
have called him Second Isaiah since we don't even know
his own name. Nebuchadnezzar had conquered Juda,
an unimportant nation in his path of violence against a

world he wanted subject to Babylon. Many years after that conquest, another warrior had risen up to triumph over Babylon in the person of Cyrus of Persia. The Jewish captives whom the Persian soldiers found in Babylon were a bedraggled lot for whom the Persians cared nothing. In the upheaval, the Jewish captives were freed and began the long journey homeward. In their joy at their newly acquired freedom and with the eyes of faith they saw the hand of God and praised their saving Lord. They looked out of their natural eyes at a few soldiers taking over their towns; soldiers who didn't care who they were or whose captives they were, or how long they had been captives. They were free to leave and to return to their own country after some fifty years of bondage.

There were among the escaping captives certain women and men who, by some mysterious gift of God's grace and love, had learned to recognize the immanence of God in daily events. These persons—and Second Isaiah was one of them—praised God who had set them free. He had leveled mountains and filled valleys so that they could go on a straight and sure path back to their home. The name of the one who freed them was Emmanuel. If we had lived at that time, we would have been saying, "The name of the one who freed you is Cyrus."

The difference is, of course, faith. Some people look out of their eyes at life and see the humdrum and the ordinary with all of its meaningless parts to endure. Others feel the same meaninglessness, endure the same struggle and duress, yet in hindsight, they see the path of God winding its way through their lives.

I want to look again at the nature of religious experience. I am a Catholic writing primarily for Catholics, yet the description of our general inability to recognize God's acts in the ordinary is a common human phenomenon.

Most of us have presumed that religious experience involves some unusual physical and/or psychic happenings. We imagine tears of compunction or burning darts of love to the heart. Erstwhile hagiographers spoke of swoons and sighs; we've read books about visions and voices. Lacking any of the above manifestations we have accustomed ourselves to thinking that religious experience is not for the common person. Better to stay away from it anyway; it is perhaps suspect or peculiar. Far safer it is to accomplish one's daily duties, live a decent life, get to Church on Sunday and see that the children go, help out at the parish spaghetti supper, volunteer for work at the local hospital, join one of the new prayer groups the parish is sponsoring—whatever. We feel very deeply both as citizens of our country and as Catholics that it is by good works that we are saved. Whatever this "faith in Jesus" business is, Catholics have not had much connection with it. We go about our works dutifully, not expecting any particular religious experiences from them, whatever they are, anyway.

Newcomers are crossing our paths offering to teach us to meditate; yoga experts sell their product. Our feeling of being on a treadmill and running from one thing to the next attracts us to the inner silence which the "do-it-yourself" meditation kits proclaim. We experience some psychological relief from meditation exercises and then feel guilty or nervous because we don't "do" the meditation exercises often enough.

Underlying the current movement to reflection is the

silent and profound summons of the Spirit of God, pointing out new paths and directions for the People of God; we, however, are slow to acknowledge the presence of God's spirit, because we haven't learned to recognize, let alone trust, the subtle activity of the Spirit of God in ordinary events. The tone of the last sentence might suggest that this book is connected with the Charismatic Movement. No. The fervent and strong devotional trend in the Catholic Church, which we have named the Charismatic Movement, is acknowledged in our scriptures. It is a devotion which has risen to prominence at other times in the history of the Christian community—sometimes to bring great good and sometimes to cause the members to form an elitist group who eventually become alienated from their sisters and brothers who seek Jesus with equal seriousness yet who are not drawn to God in this particular way.

This is a book for ordinary folks, those who usually don't see the forest for the trees in their lives. It is written for those who have some deep, basic, fundamental faith that there is God. It is for this group that I want to articulate the ordinariness, the dailyness of religious experience. It is a book about contemplation, since I truly believe that the Spirit is summoning the Church to a contemplative life understood much differently from the way we have always thought contemplation happened.

I am writing about mystery, the mystery of the power and presence of God, so very subtly and inarticulately overshadowing our lives. Most of the time we miss the obvious because we demand of mystery that it be peculiar and out of the ordinary. We do not want mystery to burden our lives, to hang heavy over our days casting some kind of cloud over our rational abilities to control and plot our destinies. The mystery seems to have cut off the pious feelings of simple devotion we knew as children. We do not want the burden of this mystery because it is just that—a burden. Our involvement in the mystery of the interconnectedness of human and divine (read: in a radical following of Jesus) warrants too total a commitment. A pleasant, socialized religious pattern lets us off the hook of scrutinizing whether our religion and our life have any connection with each other.

Yet if we are at all serious, the burden of mystery haunts our thinking and dogs our footsteps waiting for the time of interiority to come upon us. The hound of heaven waits for years sometimes until we very slowly come to the realization of the magnitude of religious commitment.

Though we hate to acknowledge the burden of the mystery of God's presence to ourselves, we know at the same time that we want the search after the face of God to be that which impels us, fascinates us and forces our days into time that is not prosaic. We hope that our religious convictions are not just a few pious secrets that we hand on to our children with something of a panicky feeling that the whole of the religious dispensation (at least that portion of it that we see to be the whole) is inadequate to address the times in which we live.

Somewhere within us, however, when we allow ourselves to ponder it, the heaviness of the presence of mystery to our lives overwhelms us and we find we need to acknowledge and, further, investigate it. We are compelled by it. Will it continue to pursue us if we run from it? Will it ever let go of us and leave us to our own puny devices? Will we be able really to cling to a world that is far too small for the desires of our hearts?

Somehow we know that within this mystery is the explanation for our lives. The mystery is the beginning and the end, the Alpha and the Omega of our days. Running after this mystery which holds the key to our ultimate identity does not make our lives any easier. In fact it seems to complicate them, yet we know that there is only one way to go if we wish for integrity. We can't escape the burden of mystery nor, in our better moments, do we wish to.

In addition, we have to deal with mystery within the pale of organized religion which so often seems opposed to mystery and in which juridical detail seems to take precedence over human development. How do we resolve the conflicts felt between personal, serious conviction and what we have learned is demanded of those professing membership in the Catholic Church? The greatest millstone around the neck of organized religion is not its authority figures but the too facile acceptance on the part of leaders and members that ritual and cult can substitute for personal commitment and for the sacrifice of one's life.

We need to examine the religious experiences and the mystery in the lives of ordinary people who would never think of themselves as contemplative persons. Contemplatives speak about their encounters with the divine in ways that are not so extraordinary after all. We need to recognize religious experiences in the matter and content of everyday with a little greater acuity.

The word contemplative conjures up images of monasteries, monks and nuns, a life of rigorous prayer or some kind of mysticism which eludes the grasp of common folks. In fact, contemplative is the name given to women and men who seek an intuitive, integrated manner of being before the Lord. The totality of their lives is focused in a unity which approximates the eternal simplicity and unity of God. This oneness resolves the multiple aspects of disintegration which each day affects the wholeness in the center of the contemplative's being. The resolution is not a repression but a hardwon human maturation interconnected with the transforming power of God's grace.

The best way to capture the meaning of a contemplative life is to draw a portrait of a person whose religious experiences have a specific character. By identifying these experiences as uniquely contemplative one can most nearly capture in human language the spirituality which for centuries we have named contemplative. The nature of this way of life has been articulated many times during the centuries; the model of contemplation offered in this book does not differ essentially from these earlier models but each generation of persons in the evolving life of the Church must translate the wisdom traditions into the terminology of the present. Otherwise, what is of great significance in a spiritual heritage can seem to have become irrelevant.

Women and men today are not asking the questions which necessitated the distinctions between natural/ supernatural; acquired/infused; ordinary/extraordinary; ascetical/mystical contemplation. Such distinctions are not unhelpful, but other approaches to the topic of contemplation have become necessary, given the varying philosophies now handmaidens to theology as well as the many social sciences which have influenced it. The last two decades have witnessed a renewal in biblical research and a resurgence of interest in the classics of Western and Eastern mysticism; both movements have contributed to the model for contemplation presently emerging.

The search into the mystery of God's summons to a contemplative life is not confined to Catholic Christians. Theologians writing on the nature of revelation show that God's epiphanies elude attempts to measure, define or control, and they are aware that the psychosomatic experiences which accompany the devout life of prayer and meditation escape doctrinal boundaries. Worldwide religious dialogue between Christians and non-Christians is possible on the level of religious experiences; however, as the movement of God into the life of humanity is defined within particular ecclesial traditions, theological diversity is obvious and necessary. Catholic contemplatives view contemplation as radically connected with God's action in history in Jesus Christ.

Jesus accepted the mystery which was at the center of his existence; the contemplative, led by the Spirit of Jesus, opens her/his life to the mystery at its center where God and humanity meet. It is the holistic search into this mystery of the interpenetration of the human and divine exemplified in Jesus which consumes the contemplative's daily existence. A contemporary model emerges as we examine the contemplative's specific modes of articulating the religious experiences of God, of Jesus, of the Church, of prayer and of all the moments of daily life—loving and communicating, working and praying, learning and changing. If we successfully trace a pattern in these articulations, we can draw an accurate portrait of the kind of human being whom God has summoned to contemplation. The manner of viewing each experience of daily life has everything to do with the contemplative person. This person is most closely in touch with daily reality and most genuinely comprehends St. Augustine's teaching that wisdom is not what is to come in the future, nor what has been in the past, but what is.

Contemplatives have known a history of misunderstanding in the Catholic Church. One need only glance at the biographies of John of the Cross, Teresa or Eckhardt to verify this. Yet the true contemplative was never a member of some elitist or arcane sect, but merely one who experienced life as more consistently integrated even in disintegrating moments. The measure of holiness is the charity of one's life, and contemplatives can be no exception to the standard. They live inside and outside of monasteries and cross all levels of society; God's summons to integration is not limited: "Through the mystery of this wine and water, may we become sharers in his divinity who humbled himself to share in our humanity."

The metaphor that most nearly approximates contemplation is integration. A former metaphor was "mystical marriage," the union of human and divine. These metaphors, though shaped by the language of different eras, suggest the same reality.

The portrait of the contemplative person drawn here fits current research in mental health and psychology. The holy individual is the healthy individual. The stress on pastoral theology evident in the Catholic Church demands that what is written and preached corroborate contemporary religious experience and that tradition be brought forward as vital truth. Thus a current description of contemplation cannot be couched in language which prevents the faithful from being able to identify with the profound summons of God to a life of integration lived out in the terms of the most ordinary and most prosaic daily experiences.

Just as for the Israelites faith was the key to seeing God's saving action in what Cyrus of Persia and his soldiers were doing in their towns, so for us Catholics faith is imperative in order that we see our times with enlightened eyes. In every experience we must learn to recognize the claim of God and know that our days are revelatory of the transcendent, always so unutterably immanent in what is simple and right at hand.

The traditional spirituality which is contemplation affords the basis for the apostolic spirituality to which many writers are urging us. Contemplation is the perfect spirituality for movement and journey precisely because it does not have to be in a monastery to happen. Because contemplation has to do with God within life, all experience becomes the locus of God's activity. Thus we do not have to go away from our lives to confront God; in fact, it is just the opposite. Sharpening the focus of the eyes of faith, we perceive God in the dimensions of the ordinary.

I have found that women more than men apprehend the language of contemplation because society has allowed its women to live more in the now, concerned with people and problems at hand. Our men have frequently had to be goal-oriented and thus often unable to be content with what is, as they must plan for what has to be. This is a situation which is changing as both women and men are being liberated from sexual stereotypes; both are allowed the kind of sensitivity necessary to be contemplative. Our sadness is that so many people refuse to allow men to be sensitive and compel them still to be an exaggerated posture of competence and strength. It is because of our societal acculturation that in their religious experience men require that Jesus be brother and friend but never Love, and that prayer be activity and tasks accomplished but never silence and nothing. It is to be hoped that the newness of the Spirit is blowing us clean of our nonsense.

The contemplative life can be described as a journey to integration. We are not speaking of navel-gazing while the rest of the world starves. Integration is not only for those who have the luxury of vacations alone at the shores or in the mountains. The integrity of our own humanity is the primary position from which we are able to recognize our own darknesses, ignorance and needs, and thus be most truly in touch with the lives of our sisters and brothers. The contemplative stance is one of presence in the midst of the world, because the contemplative is able, no matter the pain or struggle, gradually to integrate the multiple disruptions of human existence. The integration takes place deep within; we need not feel integrated but we know that we have bound ourselves steadfastly to the process of coming in touch with our own mind and of getting our lives together. By our personal efforts at integration, always overshadowed by the powerful grace of the Lord, we begin to realize that we can create the contemplative possibility in our own lives.

The theme of movement or journey to the center is a frequent allusion in literature. In Book 9 of *The Confessions,* Augustine refers to an ecstasy experience shared by his mother Monica. He employs the symbol of movement upward and speaks of advancing through all bodily faculties to the sky, then ascending farther and ultimately coming to "our own minds." The contemplative understands this progress as the journey home which Boethius describes in his *Consolation of Philosophy*. Lady Philosophy tells Boethius he must come home from the prison in which he is incarcerated, a reference not to release from prison but home to the center of his own being where the love of wisdom and philosophy exists. The pilgrimage of the contemplative life is a movement to the locus within us where we know ourselves, however inarticulately, to be rooted and grounded in God.

Augustine suggests that once one comes to one's own mind, life is wisdom, "through which all things come into being, those which have been and those which will be." He speaks of wisdom not as that which is past, nor that which will be in the future, but simply that which is. That which has been or is going to be is not eternal. The mystery of eternity defined as the now is an idea that "blows the mind" of one accustomed to live a religious dispensation which waits for this life to be over in order to be with God in eternity. The futurist ought to pray for a change of mind. Eternity has everything to do with the now and with what is in the present. To live one's life waiting for the end of it is like the family that fights and argues all the way to the Grand Canyon where the vacation is going to begin. The mystery of eternity is that it encompasses all the details of today and only by living radically involved in this day with our human energies functioning at their maximum is this time consciousness possible to us. We must begin to recognize God in what is ordinary and to live with an excitement and commitment to the loving and living of the multiple facets of what is daily.

Augustine's references to wisdom and life as what *is,* corroborates the thesis of the ordinary nature of religious experience. The traditional spirituality we have called contemplation has to do with the present. The experience of God is one of God within life, and our experience of prayer is the gradual recognition of ourselves as a contemplative presence in the world.

It is important that we do not view the contemplative person as someone outside ourselves—someone we wish to become—a product, or stationary reality out there to which we are moving as a goal. If this is our understanding then the life of contemplation will escape us because it can never be gained by some program which we can outline. We are our lives. We are presently the totality of our experiences; our spiritual lives are either radically involved with each day or they are ethereal figments of our imaginations. Our days are processive and dynamic; we need to pray to be rid of the attitude of working to become the persons we want to be in five or ten years. This statement does not exclude the need we have for mentors whose lives we admire and who offer us models of wit, intelligence and integration to which we can aspire. Hopefully, what we come to realize most about these people whose lives attract us is that though we know them to have days in which they are unstrung just like everyone else, we know them interiorly to be integrated. Our secret for becoming like them will not be by means of slavish imitation, but by the path of accepting who and what we are in the present, with a complete openness to the experiences which life will afford us to change and grow and become someone new through the years.

While we acknowledge the importance of what is and what is present, we do not thereby bless the fault and sin, the foolishness and stupidity we perceive in ourselves. Neither does the recognition of the sacramentality of the present deny us the possibility to become poorer in spirit, cleaner of heart, or a better peacemaker. But as long as we cling to the notion that the contemplative is someone out there ahead of us that we wish to become, and as long as we keep trying to solve one dilemma after the next in order to attain a contemplative presence, then more than likely we are missing the present moments with their rich promises of serendipity. Our energies are totally employed with some presumably attainable future. The way to contemplation is to love ourselves as the process which we are and to be attentive to its movements. In this way our lives are transformed into possibility of significance and celebration. Slowly we can leave behind what is insignificant and even begin to deal with the real evils in ourselves and in our society instead of with the usual illusions and foolishnesses that occupy our limited consciousness. We are able to change some of our "policies," those ancient preliminary antipathies that we set over against every new option and every new person.

It is precisely the contemplative person who knows what it means to let go of the rigid structures we have erected for how our lives will unfold. When we force our lives into narrow confines—"this relationship *will* continue in the way we determine it" or "this person must be who we demand"—we prevent the Spirit of

God from blowing us clean, from moving and creating us anew. We are afraid to sing new songs the words of which we do not know by heart. We resist change because we know nothing about the new places to which we may be summoned in our thought and of what that thought may demand in changed behaviors. Often we have a vague sense that we should listen to a certain person, or pay attention to a particular idea gained from a book, movie, or homily, but then we would have to trust. We refuse because we are afraid to move from the nest in which we have all our notions and straws neatly arranged.

When St John of the Cross tells of the dark night of the soul, he refers to the ill-ordered desires which occasion and create the darkness. The ill-ordered desires that we find most prevalent in all of us are the desires to stay where we are, to keep on playing the same songs, to refuse to grow, and to remain content, comfortable and untroubled by new ideas. The sets of circumstances in which we presently function are good enough for us. Why need we look for anything different? The ill-ordered desires of complacency—some of which are indifferent, some of which are sinful—are what create the darknesses of our lives. Obviously it is necessary to all of us that there be periods in our lives when indeed we do rest or roost in this darkness and shut ourselves up into cocoons from which perhaps new life can emerge. The darkness can hold the possibility for new creation if we make certain that we have not shut our lives off tightly in a very small vacuum sealed jar hoping that life's upheavals will not find us. We want to wrap up the pain of our lives in a napkin and bury it in a trunk in the attic so that it can never touch us again.

Ill-ordered desires for control at any cost, or for the total power to manage our affairs our way are what prevent a life of contemplation. The desire to remain stationary coupled with a refusal to trust the new person or insight, to refuse to confront our own bodily and emotional needs, or to hide from our world—all these can be cited as our most prevalent ill-ordered desires. We can choose to die in the boundaries of self-imposed shallowness or, by God's grace, we can choose to live, and to allow the violence of the pain of our lives to change us, to make us warm and human, to bring us to new depths of the possibilities of loving. We often too facilely connect the phrase "dark night" to those days in which we feel dry, exhausted and far from God. If John of the Cross is to speak to us, it seems that we might ponder a different kind of darkness which our ill-ordered desires occasion—to stand still when we are being called by God to grow, to move into our lives realistically, joyfully, seriously, totally and humanly.

The resolution of the darkness is the choice to trust another, to be open to new possibilities, to leave off tinkering with what is trivial and foolish and to move deeply into life, into God and into relationships and community with others.

Joyce Carol Oates has a poem, "After Twelve years of Travelling," in which she describes the vagabond personality, one who wanders through life with no particular directions, purposes, or relationships. One line of the poem says: "I have no face." This is a startling and pathetic admission on the part of the woman or man who floats on the surface of life and relationship, of one who has been afraid to counter life, to take it in hand and live it without mousing along in terror of the cats that might be around each corner waiting to destroy us. What usually destroys us are our own fears and prejudices that keep our world narrow and small.

There are certain external signs that allow us to recognize a contemplative person or at least to point to the possibility of the existence of a contemplative life. The contemplative person speaks about faith and life with an authenticity to which others respond. The non-contemplative is the one who mouths religious sayings or slogans but for whatever reasons, the hearer knows that the mysteries which are being preached or discussed have never touched the inner core of the speaker. The contemplative speaks unselfconsciously out of an integrity of being, continuously in touch with the day's struggles and with its happiness. The spoken word of the contemplative comes forth as a simple unadulterated wisdom that is heard deeply in the consciousness of another. Experience resonates with experience. The contemplative is not "out of it;" she/he has learned and grown from personally wrestling with the ordinary and is able to touch most deftly and accurately the pain and the joy of another.

There is a quality of single-heartedness about the contemplative. Whether married, single, or religious, the contemplative moves in a kind of one-pointed direction through life. If asked, the goal of this single-heartedness would be ultimately God, yet the observer feels as if every day of this person's life is characterized by a seriousness of purpose and direction. The symbol of the unicorn in Christianity and of the rhinoceros in the *Sutta Nipata* of the Buddhists are beautiful images of a life of integration and of a single-mindedness resulting from the resolution of ambiguity in the center of my being. The opposite, of course, is to refuse consistently to face the networks of people and situations which make demands on who I am and on what I might become if only I could be open to the infinite possibilities for growth and change with which the love of God wants to shake me from my self-chosen confinements.

The contemplative has a sharpened ability to interpret the times, thus mirroring the prophetic role in the Judaeo-Christian tradition. Contemplatives seem to have an amazing and uncanny skill for speaking just the right word in most situations, a word always simple and unpretentious. One recalls the stories of those who go in search of a holy person and await a word that the holy person would say in order to take it back, think about it, nurture it and allow it to become the transforming wisdom of their days. The holy person says: "Would you like a cup of coffee?" How badly disappointing! This one might at least have whispered some oracle-like riddle. It is because contemplatives are usually rather simply in touch with their own lives that they are able to speak to others. They do not make any foolish attempts to solve the insoluble but they seem to be able to put our perplexities into some proper focus and to speak of this with an authenticity that allows the other to respond to the evident truth of the word.

The contemplative appreciates working and praying in common with other pilgrim persons in a church group, family or religious community. The joy of being allowed spontaneity is inestimable when one is allowed to be and to rejoice in the newness of persons developing, changing and maturing. In the acceptance of one's own talents, sexuality and struggles the contemplative knows the presence and absence of God. The sign which some of the 16th century reformers saw as evidence of God's predestining—prosperity—is by no means the way the contemplative knows the Lord but rather out of the foolishness and even stupidities of the day. A sturdy house of contemplative life is being built on the moving stream of human existence.

Obsolete forms, whether of prayer or customary behaviors, give way to a quiet search for forms of life and prayer which do not stifle authentic growth or liberation of spirit. The contemplative has moved beyond the legal and the juridical, knowing always that life outraces law. Though not antinomian, the contemplative is not tied up in knots waiting to ask what to do next at liturgy or to inquire which fork to use for the salad.

The adventures of the mind summon the contemplative. Somehow we know that only by the development of one's powers of judgment and reasoning and creativity, by crafts, cooking, music, books or whatever, life and vision are expanded by the one who has opened wide all the options for the use of human potential.

These externals in some part describe the contemplative personality. In the move to integration we experience ourselves as unique and possessing great possibilities. Though we never lose the sense of our limitations and our sin, we know that others come to us and fill our emptiness as we fill theirs. We do this in some mysterious manner as a part of the Body of the Lord; we achieve that subtle communal bonding to which the People of God have always been summoned and which we are usually so reluctant and so slow to pursue. When, with serenity and tranquility, we do not look to others for directions on how to behave, what to say, or how to react, we have lost the exaggerated self-consciousness of those who are always unsure. We can be persons present to life, to its people and events; we can take an idea, see its ramifications, and deal with it in a way that is unusual and creative because we have learned to ask the further questions and to investigate the possibly new and creative thrust and direction. Our knowledge becomes gradually integrated into the totality of our lives as all outside data filters through the entirety of our existence. We do not live among piles of unrelated and ill-sorted facts. There is a sense of wholeness and harmony about the contemplative, communicated not by anything that is said but by what the contemplative person is. This is someone truly realistic but not cynical about oneself, one's relationships with others, and about all of life. It is a realism born of the experience of pain and the experience of joy.

We know that these descriptions seem to portray those who are not the bungling, troubled persons we usually feel ourselves to be. We reiterate: these contemplative persons are not persons out there or persons beyond us. It is we, ourselves, as we accept who and what we are, as we move to the deepest center of our being carrying just our reality, our talents, our abilities, and our self rooted and grounded in God. We are not anyone else. We do not seek to be anyone else. We seek to be only authentically who and what we are.

Is everybody called to the life of contemplation? Are there only certain ones in the community of the faithful and outside of the community whose lives God has compelled to integration in order that others know the immanence of God in life, a presence/absence quietly and spontaneously witnessed by the contemplative? Are contemplatives merely the saints of our world? Yes, I suppose they are—if we do not overlay the word "saint" with all its past peculiarities. The measure of holiness is always the quality of our love. We are to become the love which God *is* in a lifetime process.

Why use the word "contemplative" at all? Why not just Catholic or Christian? I have chosen this designation because I wanted to think out for myself and for others the very real possibilities of a holiness for our times which is not odd or exaggerated. The holy person, it seems to me, is the one finally able to live an exquisite balance between complete love and complete freedom— between total responsibility for our lives, our world, and our people, and total abandon and liberation in the Spirit of the Lord who leads and directs. I have chosen the contemplative as this person because in the Catholic tradition, the contemplatives fit the portrait I want to draw. I have come across many people who mirror to me what I have defined as a contemplative person. They come from all walks of life—mothers and plumbers and priests and every kind of struggler. Why are they in our midst? Does God love them specially? Sometimes a false egalitarianism gets in the way of our ability to recognize God's provident wisdom in providing ensigns for the people. If, once in a while, someone comes along who is visibly integrated, we are able to believe and to live with new strength and courage. Yet we must learn to recognize the contemplative dimensions of our own lives. These contemplative persons are ourselves as we open our lives to God's redeeming grace which heals us of the pretenses and illusions within which we like to hide.

I have chosen at the expense of correct grammar here and there to opt away from the use of masculine generic pronouns for humans or for the Lord.

I ask the reader to excuse the awkward repetitions but hope perhaps that the effect of being jarred by the awkward enables one to recognize deeply how problematic it is for women always to be referred to in masculine terms as well as how limiting it is to confine God to a masculine personality.

It is to be hoped that our language will soon admit linguistic structures more inclusive of the rest of us than has been our previous experience.

CHAPTER TWO

The Experience of God

WHEN Paul preached at Athens, he tried to reorient the religious thought of the people. They seemed a pious and interested group, yet Paul sensed that they groped in darkness for what he already knew as truth and light. He confirmed their religious sense as he tried to lead them to the worship of the God who is God. God, said Paul, is not fashioned by human hands, nor made in women's or men's images in silver, gold, or wood. God gives life and breath and is nearer to humanity than we are to ourselves, for in this God we live, move and have our being; and in Jesus, this God is revealed as incarnate in history.

This latter fact is the good news that all of us still need to hear. We have a built-in penchant for apotheosis; we like a deity that can be put on a shelf to be feared and adored, but draw back from an encounter with the God who demands that our daily life exhibit whatever it is we say we believe. The former is a safe God who can smile upon us with heart in hand, a benign aspect of divinity which is welcome, but we need to admit a God who is power exerted over our lives, power that fascinates, compels, and pursues even if we mount a horse and attempt to ride off in all directions.

Our ordinary days and the God-language we use to explain our most profound concerns need to come into focus. God's pursuit of us is most often life itself battering us with graced possibilities. We meet daily stresses and make difficult choices; only some time later do we name these happenings God, that God who over and over again drags us by the hairs of our heads to new comprehensions and new commitments to taking life seriously and living it wisely.

The awe which makes us fearful of an encounter with a demanding God countered by the fascination which draws our lives into the mystery are the two sides of the coin of our dalliances with the divine. Some days we recognize God as radically a part of our days; sometimes we wonder if there is God at all. Our search for answers is endless not because we have unflagging energies for the quest but because the God we run after is surrounded with mystery so inexhaustible that the answers elude us while the questions continue to captivate. We catch occasional glimpses of the Face which attracts, and when we decide to abandon the whole enterprise, from somewhere within us a force is exerted against our hesitations.

The meaning of these words has to be grasped in the context of making oatmeal, driving the family around, playing stickball in the streets and getting to work each day. Religious language has a specious aspect which makes us glow with appreciation in some of our halcyon moments but which comes alive only when it forms the bedrock reason for why we get out of bed each day and why we keep trying to relate to our world.

Theological assertions about God applied to our lives have been avoided in discussing the contemplative experience; instead, the significant in each day is examined to discover therein the claim of God shaping our choices and decisions. The contemplative experience of God—a specific way in which God meets humanity and the human person meets God—is not unfamiliar to many of us who try to live life seriously with some measure of reflective examination. It is an experience that is not, and should not be, static. If we live, move and have our being in God, then it stands to reason that each of us will deal with God differently and God will deal with us differently all through our lives. For whatever reasons, usually our own dullness, many of us have confined God to a particular epiphany, usually a monolith to be worshipped or neglected, but who seems to have little to do with the day-to-day. For most people God is obviously One whom they cannot very easily name, and especially so when the experience of God leaves its childhood environments and a religious vocabulary to deal with adulthood necessitates some maturation. Many then become afraid they are losing the religious heritage of their fathers and mothers, yet find that they cannot sustain a faith which does not address the present.

In order to set the contemplative experience apart from other experiences of God, I have outlined as graphically as possible some of the ways in which people who meet and know God have tried to share their experience with me. These people don't come and announce that they want to talk about God; mostly they talk about themselves, and one is fairly accurately able to discern patterns of religious experiences and the gradual developments in these that occur through the years.

The experience most frequently expressed is that of a God above us, guiding our lives and looking down either benevolently or punitively.

It doesn't take much psychology to posit that this experience corresponds with the primary relation to the parent. We pray upward with a sense of distance as vast as that between earth and sky. Although our stance is a primitive gesture acknowledging power and majesty, we usually become aware that we have a very specific sense of where God is when we pray or ponder. This basic human gesture toward the divine is the one we can make most easily; it both comforts and frightens. We can keep this God at arm's length and can ignore, control and demand except in those times when we feel destroyed or punished. Then we can react with great anger, shouting our hatred at the sky. Although this is a legitimate experience of God it can never bear the burden of explanation for the adult. The Lord leads us by different ways if we do not narrow the possibilities by a homemade and precipitous catechesis.

Thus we meet God anew as we begin to feel that distance is overcome; God is near at hand and walking beside us as friend and guide.

We know the divine proximity at least in those moments when we are feeling good about ourselves and about life. The feeling is similar to the adolescent's knowledge of the parent as no longer over against but now as friend. We turn to the benign companion on dark and painful days, sometimes to find strength, other times only abandonment, and we have aching questions about why we should be overtaken by so much pain. What has warranted the absence of God? Sometimes we simply don't care and it seems to us to be an infantile posture to be chatting with an invisible Harvey whom we imagine to walk beside us. The grappling we do with God and of God's dealing with us is all a part of a process by which, through many years, if we are open to it, God causes us to grow and to change.

We need not evaluate the various experiences of God as if one were more important than another. The words, primitive or adolescent, do not imply that we ought to advance from what is evidently a starting point. We move in and out of all of the experiences of God all of our lives; they are not a progress from first to last. On the other hand, to presume only one way is to live a life that is unexamined. I suspect most of us have never thought we might investigate our God-experiences. We do so here not to become needlessly introspective but to wonder and marvel at the providential way in which God leads us to maturation. As our life experiences change, so our experiences of God alter; we must allow for this and not try to hold on to ways of meeting God which suited us at one time but which are not commensurate with who we are becoming.

Yet another encounter with God occurs as we welcome beauty and goodness whether in people, events or nature. We are overawed by the subtleness of the sunrise and the dynamism of the sun's setting. Dawns and lakes, moonlight and rain, or the spontaneity of love or gift makes us aware that we live in an ambiance of God and that no part of our day is ever apart from this God.

As the edge of our faith is finely honed, but with a different sense of presence and power, we know that our death experiences are also encompassed within the parameters of the divine. We are never apart from the milieu of the divine whether we feel it or not. The Thou encircles our hours and our days, although we are more or less articulate about the meeting and often dependent on people and events who cause us to become aware of presence or absence. Even if we are slow in perceiving the divine surroundings, we know in our better moments a Thou who acts. As we mature in time-consciousness, we can more quickly close the gap between daily occurrences and our faith assessment of them. This integration is not an encouragement for the blithe pronouncement of ''God's will'' upon each event—a religiosity which is awkward at best since it so facilely dismisses the human struggle—but rather a growing awareness that all of our lives are lived in the context of God's reign.

Of primary importance in any of these God-experiences is a fundamental trust that through all of them, God is leading both by crooked and straight paths. We have only to sit still—which we usually do only rather nervously. Just as we try to control and manipulate our days and the people in them, so we frequently try to manipulate and confine God to the ways we think God is permitted to act. Moreover, we cannot even conceive a God who deals with us differently from the One we have scrupulously enshrined since grade school.

Spatial distance between I and Thou gives way to indwelling in a fourth experience of the divine. Persons place their hands on their hearts as they speak of God within.

I have seen only one man place his hand on his head to indicate God's presence. Although the speaker is usually unaware of the social extension, either gesture of interiority captures both the sense of God within our lives as well as God's tenting with us as a People.

The four experiences which I have singled out for identification are not mutually exclusive nor progressive in the sense that if we are "good" we will climb the ladder of ever-more-important graces. I have enumerated these four as a basic exercise toward the identification of differing kinds of religious experience. Each of us needs to locate in our own spiritual history the ways in which we have known God and in which God has been present to us. Yet the God of our daily experiences refuses to let us measure and calculate the divine entrances and exits. Through many years the ways in which we have prayed and the loci in which we have met the Lord have changed—indeed a healthy and holy growth. We must beware only of our cast-iron definition of God which forces the divine to be the analogical Father or Mother in heaven directing events as *we* would have them, albeit with a few hard knocks thrown in to keep us on our religious toes.

When we broaden our religious horizons away from our previous and pious explanations, God has broken loose from the confines which our minds imposed. The differentiation is wonderful provided we do not fear the course our lives may take if we cease manipulating to see just how far ambiguity may extend. We have worn ourselves out giving catechetical shape to the indefinable so that it will never catch us unaware and out of control.

An analysis of the previously described experiences of God allows an overall definition: There are various meetings of an I and a Thou. In the first, I am standing upon the earth countered by the heavenly Thou. In the second, the Thou has moved to a greater proximity to my life, but always retains the distance of an Other. In the third, though it has multiple manifestations, it is God who is the Thou of the sunset, the friend, or the goodness experienced. In the fourth, the Thou is known within me and within the life of the community of believers as the indwelling Thou who guides and leads.

To know the possible differences in experiences of God is essential to good human communication. Everyone does not infer the same thing when the word God is spoken. It is necessary for wives and husbands, parents and children, friend and friend, and priest and congregation to know that the content of the word often represents very different experiences. We need to find one another in the truth of each one's experience as we haltingly try to explain ourselves, or we chance missing entirely what the other person is trying to convey. We have for so long held dear and carried around with us our static notions of God that we have even presumed common understandings among everyone. It is a great advance when we understand that everyone is unique and that God reaches to save uniquely. If we pay attention to our lives from year to year, we will learn that what we mean when we say God has altered. In the darkness of faith we are on a God-journey not programmed by our own machinations but one in which we are summoned to the cloud of unknowing which will ultimately envelop our lives. When we leave off mouthing our religious explanations of everything and monitoring our days so that they conform to our preconceived notions of how religious things ought to happen, perhaps the God of surprises can intervene to teach us the broad expanse of the divine overshadowing.

The language we have used to describe God has come from centuries of piety and its theological description. Without our realizing it, however, much of the philosophical language which undergirded our religious vocabulary was exchanged for a rhetoric of process and movement. Absolute and substantive categories became incapable of explicating the mobility of our era. Without knowing what was happening in the academies of philosophy, many of us felt a kind of panic that if our God was not able to be expressed in ways compatible with our life-experiences, then perhaps there is no God or if God cannot encompass our present malaise, then possibly we need to abandon a faith which was suitable only for children. It is amazing that we have let ourselves be so egregiously shortsighted as to presume a God who is limited to our theoretical explanations or trapped by our management of the divine enterprise.

We have been forced to learn a vocabulary which can

name how God is presently acting in our midst. A very
suitable one turns out to be not new at all, but one
which has been present in the mystical and contemplative tradition in Christianity all along. God tents with
us, walks through our life with us, loves and suffers
with us not as a Thou placed somewhere spatially but as
the very depth and center of who we are and the One
into whom we are evolving. God is immanent within
and ahead of our becoming.

Our worldviews are in our bones and represent the
sum total of all our life's happenings. Until very recently, the worldview of many of us was the circum-
ference of all reality ordered by a Divine Providence
and in which we lived out our days. Though the circle
encompassed suffering and joy, nevertheless our activities were circumscribed and within definite boundaries. Somewhat abruptly the vacuum pack exploded
into an open-ended parabola whose ordering would be
accomplished by the grace and creative maturity of
those who chose to follow the Lord seriously. This
dramatic event of vast societal change forced us to
reflect on when and how God is present to us if the
corporate experience we have of God as One outside
history who oversees no longer suits a world increasingly chaotic and diverse. Although the experiences of
God which I have identified are referents against which
to measure our personal groping, we know that as a
People we are being summoned away from the God-
experiences with which we have been comfortable and
into some unknown way.

Our grandparents, parents, and many other holy and
serious people who were responsible for their world,

experienced God in the way I shall presently describe. They spoke and wrote of God with the language of one of the four experiences previously described which has sometimes made their words seem out of date and irrelevant to our present questions. But if we have trained ourselves to perceive certain clues, we will know that many of their exclamations of inability to say what they wanted coupled with their evident growth in loving identify them as saints and mystics who were very ordinary indeed. They lacked the language we now possess that helps us form our ideas and express them in processive categories. But they understood, as do we, that reality is most accurately touched, not by carefully articulating its polarities, but by coming into personal contact with every aspect of its continuum.

Thus trying to say anything at all about God has changed so radically that we find ourselves wordless as we struggle for expression. And wordless is the perfect place to be because the word which defines God also limits God.

We have a way to talk about God which is faithful to our present experience. It is an experience of God different from the previous four. The personal history of the maturation of our religious experiences and therefore the change in our conceptualizations reflected in the search for a proper language, have led the Christian community to an expression of the experience of God which is specifically contemplative.

In each prior description there is a specific locus of the divine Other. The God of the contemplative, however, is a God so radically immanent in one's human experiences of the daily that the experience of a Thou is gone beyond. The contemplative confronts an utter silence and a kind of remoteness in trying to speak of God at all. The sense of a Thou has disappeared while the contemplative tries to explain the quest after God with vague terms such as God in every day—in every dimension of life—God always—God within my life—yet not felt as a Thou or an Other.

This becomes a fearful experience for a woman or a man because it somehow hints at some carelessness in religious practice or a possible slipping off in the direction of a cavalier atheism. Yet the movement to the contemplative experience of God is essential to faith, to the interiorization of religious values, and to growth beyond the externals of cult.

If the contemplative experience of God is other than a sense of the I reaching to and being confronted by the Thou, then how is one to typify it? We are confined to the category of relationship whenever we try to think, talk about, or pray to God. Presumably we have no intellectual tool with which to think of God outside the conceptual framework of a relationship between an I and a Thou. Merely to suggest another articulation of the connection between God and humanity perhaps hints at madness or, God forbid, pantheism.

Risking these difficulties, I offer the category of identification. One quickly dismisses the pathology of inventing a false personality, e.g., "I am Napoleon." Simply, and without entering the lists of various disputes, I maintain that there is a gradually developing sense in many that they are filled with the fullness of God as the Epistle to the Ephesians promises:

> May Christ dwell in your hearts through faith, and may charity be the root and foundation of your life. Thus you will be able to grasp fully, with all the holy ones, the breadth and length and height and depth of Christ's love, and experience this love which surpasses all knowledge, so that you may ATTAIN TO THE FULLNESS OF GOD.

We hear religious words and sentences so often that we usually let them become commonplace. We should welcome the people who can translate faith into a religious language which speaks to every day. Otherwise so great a disparity occurs between our lives and our religious explanations and assessments of them as to give the impression there is no connection whatever. The transforming grace of the Lord can bring our words and our daily praxis more and more into congruence. If our faith development is not commensurate with our human maturation, or if in fact our religious development is co-extensive with our human growing but we have no theological vocabulary which can express the focus, we will probably put our faith heritage on some closet shelf to be vaguely respected but hopelessly outdated. In his novels and plays John Powers has shown us how easily this can happen.

The experience of God we name God-within-life is a different human experience from God experienced as Thou, however or wherever spatially conceived. It is an experience we are in touch with the more truly and certainly we are in touch with ourselves. What follows is an attempt to say as simply as possible the way a contemplative knows God.

Truth is one of the names given to God. Instead of letting this name float majestically far from our ordinary situations, we can extend its significance so that we perceive it as somehow radically connected with the progressive truth of our own existence. As the truth of self gradually overcomes what is inauthentic and inconsistent in us, we move to that Truth which God is. The process takes a lot of honesty and willingness to live with our minds open, in order to let go of some of the defenses in which we hide from ourselves and others.

If we live always ready to seek anew the face of the Lord, the truth of self will emerge to replace the deceits. There is much in each of us that is silly and superficial, dark and even evil. Life batters against us with its inexorable illogic. So much that happens is absurd—miscommunications, unnamed depressions, people problems, family tragedy of one sort or another as well as deep moments of joy, love, meeting, friendship, and growth. The fabric of each day offers much that is fearsome and always much that is beautiful. We can pick and choose among our experiences sifting out the ones with which we do not wish to deal and repress the information or situations we wish to avoid. We can shelter ourselves, refuse any challenge, and content ourselves with partial truth. But if we let truth grow in us, then God is that truth in and by which our lives eventually become authentic.

Life's blows take many forms. Some are small, yet annoy or hurt us. Some cause us to be down-hearted or to lose any zest we might have to move through the day. Sometimes it's so trivial an incident as the pot being left on the stove (once again) by a careless member of the family who never washes a dish. More often it is the mis-hearing and mis-reading of another's words or intentions and the slow, killing lack of meeting that wastes our human energies. Even greater are the serious tragedies of illness, death, separation which is irreparable, or the breakdown of any possibility of being clearly understood by someone whom we care very much to have understand us. The global sinful situations—calculated deprivations and deceits—cause us to know a kind of powerlessness and the futility of our words and actions. We can choose to protect ourselves with small visions which absolve us from responsibility.

In each human crisis we can contrive ways to seal ourselves off from the change it would require of us if we faced life squarely, absorbing both its joy and its pain. Easiest of all is the option to disclaim interconnectedness, to remain smug in our behavior patterns and, of course, never to change our minds. If these are our decisions, then we shall never become truth; we will never know the experience of contemplation for we have successfully sheltered ourselves from truth by our decisions for falsehood, pettiness, superficiality, and shallowness. The hurts we might have to endure if we expanded our consciousness might be more than we could sustain. It is safer to keep our lives manageable. But God is Truth and when we hide from truth, we miss that Immanence which works to pulverize our preliminary antipathies in order to let us be free, new, and open to the possibility of personal truth. If we open our lives to development and learn whatever there is about ourselves that is shallow and in need of grace—then we will meet God each day, in each situation that opens us to ourselves and at once to Truth. The movement to the truth of ourselves, at once a movement to God who is the Truth of which our truth is radically a part, is one aspect of the contemplative's experience of God.

Wisdom is another of God's names. Many passages in the scriptures portray this aspect of God. My favorite is the following from the Book of Wisdom:

> For in Wisdom is a spirit
> intelligent, holy, unique,
> Manifold, subtle, agile,
> clear, unstained, certain,
> Not baneful, loving the good, keen,
> unhampered, beneficent, kind,
> Firm, secure, tranquil,
> all-powerful, all-seeing
> And pervading all spirits,
> though they be intelligent, pure and very subtle.

With the juxtaposition of many powerful words, the God who is wisdom is described in feminine terms. This poise of the Infinite offers another possibility for articulating the contemplative experience of God.

One of the ways in which we judge human maturation is by the presence of wisdom. It is a beautiful and grace-filled event when in a family, religious community, or parish we come upon those wise ones upon whom the community seems to be founded and who have become its wisdom teachers. Unfortunately it is often our experience that persons age as shallowly and cynically as they behaved at eighteen. Yet in some we witness a wisdom born of life lived to its fullest. As the various disintegrating life situations occurred, these persons were able to integrate and resolve ambiguities in the center of themselves. Their wholeness did not mean they "had it all together" all of the time. Wise people are easily able to communicate their experiences of disruptions—disruptions of relationships, of ideas, and the personal disruptions deep within. But through it all they were moving toward human-divine maturation. God summoned them. They responded. They became wise in the God who is Wisdom and in whom the entire process of human maturation was taking place.

It is not the wise ones who always have all the answers; it is their splendid ability to formulate the questions that draws us to them. Theirs is the gift to be open to a person with a different expression of wisdom; theirs are the minds always available to another facet of the God who is wisdom. Compassion, serenity, and an ability to accept even the most unacceptable persons and situations seem to characterize the person of wisdom. When they speak, their words bear the mark of the suffering that led them to wisdom. They deal with situations without the issues being cluttered by the personal rages and angers that betray the entrepreneur who is out for personal gain. Anyone who searches for wisdom can find these people because like calls out to like. As the wisdom of their lives matures, they know quite surely that God is that Wisdom which they are becoming.

This is yet another way to describe the contemplative experience of God. It is not the occurrence of one day, but the process of a whole lifetime. The prerequisite is an openness to the complexity within each day as the multiple details shape wisdom by God's grace or destroy the creative possibility provided within personal freedom. As each bit of differentiation from the usual plateau experiences occurred, the wise ones embraced life, discounting nothing and welcoming the advent of God however it occurred. Because of this continuing process, and because of God's graces, they somehow began to share God's nature—they became what God is —wise. And it is evident to us outsiders. We have some uncanny sense which distinguishes one who is wise from the newcomer who has arrived to foist ponderous notions upon us with the beginner's naivete.

Wisdom happens in some, and when it does, it causes all of us to rejoice. We suspect that this is not a chance phenomenon but is co-extensive with the response of those persons who in the monotonous or exciting routine of each day become contemplative. That this aspect of God is described in the scripture in feminine terms should undoubtedly give us a hint that what we need so desperately in the Church today is the presence of just this wisdom as it is integrated in the lives of the men and women who are sensitive enough to know that most often life outraces law. This feminine wisdom which describes the nature of God and which is resident in us is needed to temper the far too aggressive and masculine characteristics by which both women and men in the church calculate to make history happen. The contemplative man or woman knows the feminine in God and the feminine in themselves in that perfect equilibrium which is the nature of the androgynous God.

Another avenue by which to examine the contemplative experience of God is to bring God's name—Life— into convergence with life as each of us experiences it daily. Life challenges and demands of us. We are free to close our ears and live right at the surface rejecting any relationship or circumstance that might cause us to think a new thought, play a new piece, or get a new hairstyle. With a brash narrowness we function at eight percent of our human potential.

We can, however, face the unexpected alterations of the way we had determined our paths would go, and by God's grace, live again through the devastations that could cause us to choose death forever. The choice of life or death is very real. Living takes so much effort; dying allows us to close ourselves off from any further hurts or changes. But if we choose life, then God is that life that summons us forward, that makes demands of us and that causes us to change. All of a sudden, our life begins to take shape within the context of God's life. No part of our lives is separated from the Lord; however, this experience of God is most often nothing and nowhere. We seem to walk without God, yet the divine dogs our footsteps. Occasionally there are eruptions of God into our lives, and we are forced to make some faith assessments of our days. We have no answers for the kind of strange things that befall us and demand so much of us. Unlike the popular song which says: "You surround yourself with people who demand so little of you," God never demands little of us. It is we who are content to shuffle along getting by with as little of life and experience as we possibly can. But if we live vigorously, the new life that becomes ours is none other than the life of God.

Sometimes life can exhaust us with its advents and surprises. Couldn't one day ever be just like the last? We suspect that such differentiations are in fact the provident God, though not named by us in the immediate experience, pushing us a little farther each day, if we let life happen to us. For the contemplative, life is never prosaic or monotonous because nothing happens quite the same way twice; nor does anyone approach us, whether a very dear loved one or a stranger in quite the same way on any two days.

I must stress again the very ordinariness of all that I am saying. Often, when compared to religious people, the contemplative feels like the village atheist. The contemplative sees life in very ordinary terms; religious people somehow feel compelled always to explain it. The contemplative is able to walk down the street, buy a newspaper, sit in the park, speak at a meeting, go to church, visit a neighbor, and walk the dog without any particular need to tell God about it or thank or praise God. The contemplative is a praise of the glory of God but all of this in such ordinary ways and within ordinary days.

In the literature of the contemplative tradition we find the writers struggling to speak of their experience of God. They insist that they have no words, that this is an experience which is unutterable. Silence is the only useful language. Inaccessible, incomprehensible, are the adjectives which the contemplative uses to describe the meaning of God in life. Instead of letting these words connote a Transcendent beyond any of our powers of imagination, perception, love or search, I want us to face the fact that most of life is unutterable. In its most painful situations, the best language is silence. When our friends suffer, when tragedy gathers all of us in its inevitable hold, the rhetoric of consolation begins to sound inane and banal. It is the time for silence. It is the time for wordless healing. Faith is imperative to the one who knows that it is God-who-acts in these details of life for which we have no words. When we come to pray and our experience of meeting is a nothing experience in which we feel only knots of depression and distraction, the wordless emptiness which surrounds us with its remoteness is perhaps the silent antechamber of the divine, the entrance to the cloud of unknowing, or the apex of the mind about which mystics and contemplatives write. Must we always presume that the contemplative life is completely unlike our own?

Gregory Nazianzus said of God: "You are the end of all. You are One. You are all. You are Nothing. You are not One. You are not all." These mysterious paradoxes describe our days of all and nothing. God's presence within our lives is all and nothing. Apophatic language has always been the best tool the contemplative knew to catch a glimpse of a mystery beyond all grasping of mind, heart, or daily experience. If there is anything the contemplative knows in her/his better moments, it is that the whole crazy business of God's presence within life is as real and everywhere as it is nothing and nowhere.

Apophasis lets those who can, touch the mystery of God's presence more faithfully. By this rhetorical tool the mind is compelled beyond the affirmations of God, such as kindness or mercy, into a wilderness which is fearsome to the beginner. Those whom the Lord summons to contemplation, however, recognize the territory of unknowing and in fact breathe a sigh of relief to be away from facile replies to the interminable questions. The need to have everything neatly packaged was forsaken long ago by the contemplative who recognizes that most often it will be murky ambiguity which will surround much of life. A kind of merriment replaces the feeling of dragging boulders up the sides of human contrariness—a merriment often the best disarmament of the somber or of the hypocrites who feel that gloom is the only attitude with which to appear serious.

The thought of God is certainly not always present to the mind of the contemplative, nor is the contemplative a Pollyanna, mouthing religious slogans to suit each troublesome occasion.

It is usually in hindsight that the contemplative begins to realize how, through all the pieces and parts of life, God has been consistently dragging us along. We did not make a life-plan at age 14 which outlined how to act in each threatening affair. Instead, without our comprehending what was happening to us, we were moved ahead a notch, we grew, we understood new insights and changed in very miniscule and very great ways. All of this movement, the contemplative knows, is God within life. Grace was present to pull us forward to yet another phase of human growth in that wisdom and truth of God that we are becoming. This is the contemplative's perception of the category of identification and is the particular way in which this human being experiences and proclaims God.

The mystics have always been accused of seeing everything as one, and that is indeed what the contemplative personality does. So advanced is the degree of their integration of the ambiguities of life that all fragmentation comes together in the One which God is. To the degree that this integration is taking place in a human person by God's grace, so is that individual drawn into the life and heart of God.

The identification is felt in a kind of quiet wonderment, touched occasionally in reflective times. We are not as we were one year, five years, or ten years ago, and all of the differentiation is involved in the great mystery of God's love. The contemplative is usually without words to account for this happening, yet has strong convictions that indeed this experience of God is as it is. It is not reserved to monks and nuns in contemplative monasteries. Oddly enough, some people in monasteries are not contemplatives at all, but rather rigidly legalistic folks who put in their dutiful times of prayer and labor. There is not much sense of the radical immanence of God to and within their lives. God is always someone outside of their reality to Whom they turn with prayers, requests, and information about themselves and their days. They praise and proclaim but to a God who is not within the fabric of each day.

On the other hand, there are contemplative persons inside and outside monasteries. These are the ones who over a long period of time know God in life, an experience which does not negate other experiences of God nor other ways of addressing God in prayer. Contemplatives praise and proclaim, celebrate liturgy and express concern for their world and its peoples, yet these prayers arise from a totally different stance and a totally different way of viewing reality. If God is experienced within life, then one does not go outside life to find God. Faith grows deep and strong in the redemptive possibilities of each day. The instances of redemption are small and large, stupid or wonderful, because life has no defined parameters. In hindsight, the joys, the small troubles, or the large painful blows are all seen to be the warp and woof of redemption.

It is not possible to state this life in a few words. It is rich and full; it has its low times and its complexities.

But none of life is, for the contemplative, apart from God. Absence and presence begin to be the same. Absence is painful; presence is joy-filled; yet God is present in both experiences. Absence is finding the sticky pot on the stove. There is no God and nothing in that experience, just as there is no God and nothing in the experience of the death of a loved one or in the pain of a break in communion with a friend. We are bereft, but someone comes along with a tunafish casserole and in some small way, we know once again that there is God and that this God, whose face we do not see, acts to save. We have been dragged along again.

CHAPTER THREE

The Experience of Jesus

THE experiences of Jesus for Christians vary as do our experiences of God. We know Jesus in the stories told of him in the scriptures; we know his words through the readings we have heard through the years; we know Jesus present in sacrament, and through prayer; we know Jesus in the midst of the community of believers; we have had the experience of his presence and absence in our lives. We have known days when it is fairly easy to understand what following him might be all about and we know other days when the entirety of Christian faith has been merely the word "Catholic" in the blank marked "religion."

Often, experiencing Jesus has been insignificant or even suspiciously Protestant compared both to the magisterial and the popular emphasis on ritual and on a moral life. Yet many of us are feeling that cult, which should sacramentalize the presence of Jesus in the community, is often mere external form and motion. If we reflect at all, we perhaps incipiently recognize that cultic celebration has to have some connection with the following of Jesus. Ritual should arise out of life and return to grace it. On our better days we long to connect our daily choices with our call to discipleship. Somewhere along the line we know that we do not act morally because of law but because the following of Jesus demands a particular kind of lifestyle.

The Second Council of the Vatican called for a renewal to ground our faith again in the person of Jesus. We had gotten far away from experiencing ourselves as disciples of the Lord and many voices were calling us to change. We pray for enough dynamism and grace to force us from the apathy that rejects freedom and embraces the magic, miracles and authority about which the Grand Inquisitor warned Jesus in the powerful scene from *The Brothers Karamazov*. Both in the novel and in reality, we want to run from the arduous tasks of faith and personal responsibility to content ourselves with a non-challenging spiritual praxis.

The mysterious summons of the Spirit calls us to reexamine our religious experiences of Jesus and to embrace a life of discipleship. A tamed religion is too small for our hearts and minds, and we search for, though repeatedly draw back from, a faith that demands everything that we are. If we scrutinize our own life process and identify our gradual awakenings to the meaning of the Lord, we will realize that the Lord Jesus is present and that his word is as effective today as it was when the first followers abandoned whatever held them back from apostleship.

Meeting the Lord is a human process and we need some reflective time to ascertain the development of our faith and of our commitment to Christianity, however vaguely religious we may have assessed these to be. Once we are brought by grace and choice to the contemplative experience of Jesus, there is no return, though we may lack a proper language to name the encounter and are usually dependent upon our prior, and often outdated, religious vocabulary.

The contemplative seeks God primarily in the human because of the profound mystery of incarnation, and in Jesus life takes on a very specific meaning. His community of disciples still attracts those who can grapple with paradox: life in death, light in darkness and power in weakness. Though denial of self and the embrace of the cross has often been a refuge for self-rejecting neurotics or a tool of oppression for the unscrupulous, nonetheless, the absurdity of sacrificial love captivates us with godly power to demand that life be given for the friend and love be offered an enemy.

In Jesus, that which is divine and inaccesible to us became a man; God became what we are. Thus forever, in the empowerment of the Spirit, humanity contains the possibility of beholding the divine dimension in itself. No other religious dispensation calls its followers to such a radical embrace of humanity as does the Christian. Though it is a commonplace notion to the average Christian for others to believe that what is divine became human is unthinkable. However proximate other religious groups may determine their God to be, none makes this extraordinary claim of radical immanence and of identification between humanity and divinity. The idea should leave us breathless, yet Catholics don't really like to deal with this mystery very much. Like any other religious group, we place our god on a shelf, safely removed from making much impact on our lives. That we are to embrace the human and the daily the way God has done in Jesus requires too much of who we might have to become. Yet this is the meaning of Christian faith.

We need to get in touch with our experiences of Jesus, tracing the salvific movements through our years and recognizing that the image of Jesus was being carved in us by the Spirit of God. Closing the gap between each day and our faith assessments of it is a primary task of the maturing believer. Our initial experience of Jesus was that moment in which we knew unerringly that our turning to the Lord was no longer dependent upon the faith of parents or community. Jesus, and the details of his life recorded by the Christian community through their personal faith experiences, began to become the foundation of our lives. The conversion took place in many ways—a person, a book, an event awakened a faith that earlier was only a mirror of others' beliefs. Now, Jesus becomes real for us personally. In some inchoate way his message and its meaning for us becomes apparent.

This first meeting was historically situated, that is, we began to know Jesus as he was when he lived upon the earth. We wanted to imitate him, to listen to his teachings and to become followers. An illustration similar to those in the previous chapter portrays the believer looking back in time and space to Jesus, a picture meant to convey our sense of distance from and yet meeting with Jesus.

These conversions happen in very ordinary circumstances. No particular age is essential nor does the setting of the conversion have to be religious. At age 14, we may decide without any great explanation to ourselves that we ought to stop fighting with our brothers and sisters. We have some vague notion that the Christian life demands something better of us than the constant haggling we have been doing. Perhaps we have no religious words for this change nor do we carry it out very well; nevertheless, a change has occurred that is more than a sibling truce. Unknown and inarticulate to us, there was a movement of God's grace which caused us to alter even one small detail of our lives.

We may decide during college that we can't fritter away our time; there is a world of hungry people around us who lack even minimal housing or employment. We get involved in certain school projects that demand something more of us than shooting pool at the student union. Such ordinary human growths are authentic religious experiences whether we acknowledge them or not in the moment of their happening. God has acted in our lives; we are beginning to live more consciously aware of what it means to be at once human and Christian. If our religious worldview excludes the ordinary, then these two instances probably remain unnamed and undefined. But if we examine our life-journey with some seriousness, we can trace the footprints of the Lord, albeit in the shifting sands. We have been forced out of a static existence, although many times we may have fought the processes of maturation. Other and greater conversions will take place through the years ahead. But these early experiences or similar ones awakened something in us. We had to make our own the faith of our parents and of the Christian community. We ourselves must confront the Lord and live with awareness and purpose according to the Gospel message. Hereafter, in some ways, however miniscule at first, our lives will be evaluated by the metaphor of discipleship announced in the Christian scripture.

But this initial experience of Jesus is merely that—a beginning. The Christian has yet a long way to go from the introductory encounter, with its call to imitation, to the final point of identification with the Lord Jesus. A second stage in conversion is our discovery that the distance between our lives and that of Jesus in his own era is overcome. Jesus escapes the boundaries of human chronology and is present as friend, brother, savior, guide, exemplar and director of our lives.

We know Jesus as present in sacrament, in meetings, and in prayer when two or three are gathered in his name. We know him in the person who asks for food, water, clothing, or shelter. We know the presence of Jesus to the Church. We pray to the Lord who walks with us through our lives—sometimes absent in our feelings, sometimes present.

The contemplative experience of Jesus is, however, yet a different experience and is the highpoint of the Christian's conversion. "I have been crucified with Christ, and the life I live now is not my own; Christ is living in me. I still live my human life, but it is a life of faith in the Son of God, who loved me and gave himself for me." This sentence from the Epistle to the Galatians nicely captures the contemplative experience of Jesus, one beyond the experience of relationship. Identification has become the essence of my understanding of Jesus Christ. The sketch of two has become one.

The Experience of Jesus

Our first inclination is to think that we become like Jesus when we feel good about ourselves. If we see ourselves becoming kinder, more generous or tolerant of others, we might have a fleeting thought that we are approaching more nearly the mind of Christ. Most often we excuse ourselves, saying that the imitation of Christ is for saints and that we, who are sinful and weak, must stand on some lower rung of the ladder where the demands are fewer. Some persons might turn out really well—some holy, elderly ladies or dedicated lay families who attend cursillos or make marriage encounters, or a few priests, brothers or sisters, but not us regular types. What we need to know from the outset is that identification with Jesus has nothing to do with how we might be feeling about ourselves and about the merit of our days. Paul's explanation of identification with Jesus was by no means to be equated with a self-achieved holiness.

Both by citizenship and religious training, we can't get free of the notion that we have to pull ourselves up by our bootstraps even in religious matters. The reverse side of this coin is that we can flagellate ourselves verbally and mentally if we do not measure up to what we might become if we tried. We have the idea that there is nothing we can't do if we have the book of directions. The Church was responsible for its printing and we can heap burning coals on our heads for "not getting at it" when we know we should. This particular script is a wonderful subterfuge to disclaim responsibility for discipleship. We can always beat our breasts while the real issues of our world are unattended.

The identification which Paul knew to be the height of the Christian experience of Jesus, came to Paul as it comes to us, only in one way: Every day we must die with Jesus and every day we will live with Jesus through the transforming power of God. Now, living and dying, as we saw in the previous chapter, is something very daily and prosaic. It consists in all sorts of puny experiences which annoy, hurt, or plague us as well as larger experiences which confuse, overwhelm, or threaten to destroy us. We find things within ourselves that we cannot straighten out no matter how hard we try. Where does the superficiality in us come from? Where the smallness of vision? Where the pettiness, the bleak depression, not to speak of the rages and hatreds which have us by the throat? There is in us that which is incomprehensible, which springs out of us with some fearsome results when we least expect it. There is the inability to name our own feelings even to ourselves.

How explain the external pieces of life to us that are absurd—the injustices which defy our best efforts at reform—war and armament, unpeace everywhere, the violence within and outside ourselves? We want different and better times, but neither we nor many of our neighbors, local or global, seem able to turn desires and talk into reality. There is that inexorable law in our flesh which wars against the law of our minds. Why do we not do the good we desire but rather the evil which we despise? Why is so much of life out of focus? Why does injustice have the upper hand?

A zen koan gives a plausible insight to begin the clarification of these questions. The master offers a riddle to the disciple who has come seeking wisdom. "What is the sound of one hand clapping?" Beginning disciples are usually overeager and this one is no exception. The disciple is not displeased with the task at hand and puts an immense amount of rational energy into the task of solving the riddle and unraveling the inner core of its meaning. Many times over the master is compelled to correct the self-satisfied efforts of the disciple. If one may be allowed a hypothetical conclusion to this story: Many years later (read, experiences) the disciple, chastened by life, approaches the master with a wisdom that has learned to confront the absurd, not to resolve it. The conversation is not an analysis of one hand clapping but rather a simple invitation: "Let us drink tea together."

What does tea have to do with the absurd? In the face of all the conflicts within and outside of ourselves, we finally learn that we cannot make rational that which is irrational, nor make sensible that which does not make any sense. What is, is. What is important in this moment of meeting of master and disciple is not explanations but the embrace of the present moment in sharing a cup of tea.

Life is absurd. We are most often in the midst of many confusions. "If only things had not gone this way," or "This situation is so dumb." Our initial response to the absurd is to change it and to force it somehow to make sense. And of course, it never does. When we stop trying to manipulate life and stop figuring out how to prevent the absurd, we come to know that wisdom is simply to stand before the absurd, never denying who and what we are, and die the way Jesus died in the face of the ultimate absurdity of the cross.

To stand before the absurd and die means that we

shift into a different gear to deal with the situation or person at hand. We change. The pain of the moment does not dissipate in this choice. But by the transforming power of grace we are enabled to move beyond the dying experience. With the eyes of faith, we slowly and painfully recognize that we have been empowered to live again if indeed we choose life and not death.

To stand before the absurd and accept the deaths it will cause us—the deaths of our own notions about things, the deaths of our own pretenses and illusions, deaths even of our most sacred and important ideas and commitments—does not mean letting life wash over us as if we were rocks in the sea. We are summoned by the church people to take seriously the task of social justice, particularly in regard to systems changes. We are not permitted merely to view our own stupidities and content ourselves that we have no responsibility to turn things around in our world.

But the absurd dimension of life is never far from us. We have to put on the mind and attitudes of Jesus. He preached and taught the meaning of God and life as he uniquely and supremely understood all truth. The religious people of his time rejected his understanding of God, named it blasphemy, and ultimately, because he would not alter who and what he was, and what he stood for, death by crucifixion became the inevitable consequence of the way he chose to live his life.

There are many small absurdities in each day, mostly our own set ways pitted against the set ways of the various people who inhabit our lives. "Are you going to wear *that?*" "Do you always make your spaghetti sauce *this* way?" As our usual controls are thwarted, we will be forced to move or change one way or another. Either we can open our lives to the new and possibly fuller dimension or we can close off any new information that would upset our carefully arranged plateaus.

These smaller conflicts pale in comparison with the absurdities that threaten everything we are—separation, death, miscommunication, breakup of relationships, illness, and finally the gradual diminishment of our human faculties as we approach physical death. Beyond our personal sufferings is the knowledge that corporately—by the lifestyle we continue to demand—we bear responsibility for the hunger of the world, for massive unemployment, and for the imminence of war. We feel that we must stand for justice over against forces so gigantic and so intrinsically evil that we weep tears of impotence to determine any meaningful course of action; mostly we weep because we can stand beside the pain of the world as we watch it on television and recognize that we have become inured to the plethora of it. The pain of the world's problems doesn't last long enough in our consciousness to cause us to hunger and thirst after justice. We see ourselves hungering and thirsting only for the pizza during the commercials.

These are some of the names of the absurd; each one of us can add further examples. In the presence of the absurd, we are forced to die, that is, to change, to alter behavior patterns, sometimes to see our most cherished ideals trampled by enemies whose rigidity, pettiness of vision, and personal insecurities cause our spirits to falter. Something inside us dies. If we recollect our minds and recall the trail of the absurd throughout our lives, we may begin, in faith, to perceive the presence of the death-resurrection mystery of Jesus as it continues in the lives of his followers.

Barbara Doherty

All humankind has ups and downs; Christians have no corner on the market. But the paschal mystery has invested the ups and downs of daily life with redemptive significance. The absurd is weighted with the salvific possibility. This does not imply that in the moments of the absurd of life, we blithely set aside its anguish or terror by a religious platitude but rather that as we look back through the years, we can see how we have been able to continue rather than to die forever. Continuing —simple human continuing—is the meaning of resurrection.

Indeed, the way we come to identification with Jesus is not when we feel good about ourselves, but only when we have died many times and have been raised up many times by the lifegiving power of God. "Every day I die and every day I am raised up." This is the meaning of baptism. As we die and are raised up each day, we move from imitation of Jesus to identification with him. Our life is the redemptive life of Jesus lived out in the context of our world in its present history.

An immense faith is, of course, required of us as it was required of Paul to believe that these words are true. The power of God constructs our lives. The difficulty with most of us is that we are always looking in the wrong places and times for our religious experiences. The power of God leads, directs and transforms in the everyday, in the prosaic, in every single occurrence of each day, but we have been trained to look only for the unusual happenings and the unusual people like Dorothy Day or Thomas Merton. These are the "heavies," as one national magazine called them. We surely have no experiences of God or Jesus similar to these people's. And while we are looking at them and at their experiences of living the Christian life, we miss all the manifestations of God within our own.

The power of God which transforms us is that ability given us beyond our own natural bursts of energy to continue on after some devastating experience has knuckled us under or to begin anew when something trivial has upset us. If we investigate the pattern of such experiences in prayerful reflection, we can see rather easily that in fact, it has not been our own thought that has saved us, but once again, God has acted to save. We enter now into a new phase of our human maturing. We have passed over from death to life, a new life—one now beyond, different from, more enlarged than, the one which we knew before.

This resurrected life is to be distinguished from natural zest. There is a power beyond our own which has lifted us up to start again. The power of the resurrection experience does not change the pain of the death, no more for us than it did for Jesus. The pain and the ugliness of dying and human pain are still present to our consciousness and may linger there until time causes a natural healing process. Yet healing has occurred and we know it. We have been raised up. We continue living, but now with a new life. The quality of this new life is other than that which we knew prior to the paschal moment. We know ourselves to be dealing with our lives now in terms of faith. We are enabled to say, "it is the Lord" to the details of our days, at least in hindsight.

The accounts of the resurrection of Jesus in the scriptures don't give us much help. Why didn't those who knew Jesus and loved him not recognize him after the resurrection? Only those whose faith eyes were sharpened knew him. We need to learn the same lesson or else we too fail to name the transforming power of the God-events of our lives.

Words are so inadequate to convince us that we must pray for a faith that embraces all of the details of our human struggling and striving. It takes us so long to recognize the love which causes us to change our ways and our minds and which over many years carves out in us the image of the Son. We are to become one with Jesus. Augustine tells us that it was only when he began to see divinity in the weakness of Jesus, that he truly began to know the Christian mystery. It is not only the weakness of Jesus to which Augustine refers, but our own weakness in which we await the transforming power of God. But this happens in instances so ordinary that we overlook our religious experiences and plod through each day without so much as a shred of faith to assess events.

The contemplative person is the one who knows the ordinariness of religious experience most certainly. The sacred and the secular are not two but one. God has embraced all of creation. It is we who must learn to behold in this day—this person, this stupid detail, this argument, this joy, this meal to prepare, this talk with someone on the phone, this growth and change, this work for justice with its small success and its innumerable setbacks—all of these are the means of identification. It is now no longer we who live but Jesus. We become Jesus in our world. Not because we think we look or act like Jesus but because we die and are transformed, too, and our lives are redemptive.

We live the life of Jesus embracing the consequences of that commitment. Perhaps the cross will be the eventuality of our choice as it was for Jesus. As our commitment becomes more deeply ingrained, it will force us to decisions and ways of acting that will perhaps be unpopular. It may be that friends and relatives will have to set us aside because we have begun to threaten a socially acceptable religious lifestyle. The commitment made in our baptism begins to take significant shape and to require that we become follower in every dimension of our beings. The call to discipleship has mysteriously summoned us and we recognize now there is no turning back.

Anselm's question "cur deus homo" perennially plagues us: why the God-man? What are the implications of this mystery for us? To investigate the issue, Karl Rahner, in an inimitably brilliant fashion, begins his theological process by discussing not what God is but what humanity is. His definition refers to us as an indefinability which comes to consciousness of itself. We can define a good deal about ourselves yet we know a mysterious core which we cannot name, a core which is indefinable and usually inexpressible. At the center of our subjective selves is that which causes us to wonder at our own goodness and that which causes us to fear what can get out of control. Rahner speaks of the lifetime task of accepting or rejecting our indefinabilities. He shows how Jesus did this to such an eminent degree that he in his humanity became of the very nature of God.

The promise of divinization is held out to us. We have proclaimed for centuries in our Eucharistic celebration that Jesus became a partaker of our humanity in order that we might become partakers of his divinity. Such a statement would be pretentious if it were not the central focus of Christian revelation. Whatever else we may understand theologically, the Christian believes that the divine and the human are forever interpenetrated in Jesus and causal to that interpenetration for us adopted daughters and sons of God.

What does becoming a partaker of divinity feel like? It is enough of a struggle trying to become human. However, as we become more truly human, at the same time and co-extensive with that process, we are becoming divinized. That maturation is what our ordinary lives are all about. Most of the time we miss the significance of the daily because we are always waiting for dramatic situations to arise in which our mettle can be tested and we will rise gloriously to some extradorinary demand.

Most of the time we have limited the meaning of baptism to a cleansing from original sin which wiped the slate of our soul clean and allowed us to escape limbo and gain heaven. Often we have viewed baptism as a kind of entrance requirement into the club. Both these childhood notions contain truth: To be baptized into the death and life of Jesus does overcome the estrangement that humanity has from the divine, and our baptisms do place us within the community of those who enter into the mystery of living a Christian life. But what it means to be baptized is so profoundly relevant to our consciously becoming Christian, that we must reinvestigate it in order to recognize its powerful presence in daily life.

The epistle to the Romans tells us that we are baptized into the death of Jesus so that we might live the life of Jesus. This faith statement has to be taken from the shelf of our stored-up religious notions and be seen to be connected with the deaths and transformations that occur daily. The reality of the sign of baptism, though a profound change in our ontological meaning, is also co-terminous with our human development. It is only through many years that we understand what dying and rising is all about, let alone grow in the belief that our ordinary life process is redemptively significant.

The writings of the Fathers of the church indicate that they discerned the spiritual progress inherent in the "becoming" of a Christian. St. Justin tells us that by baptism we move from being children of needs and ignorance to being daughters and sons of free choice and knowledge. He refers to baptism as enlightenment because those are inwardly enlightened who finally learn these truths.

Anyone with even a modest amount of life experience knows that in the ontological twinkling of an eye, the catechumen is not enlightened and utterly capable of making free choices. Our psychological knowledge has greatly increased since Justin's day, yet his language intimates a process of dynamism and movement which baptism sacramentalizes. In faith the baptized individual gradually makes choices out of a mind and heart that become increasingly enlightened about the meaning of a Christian way of life. The mystery of dying and transformation is part of each day.

Clement of Alexandria corroborates the processive tone of St. Justin. He speaks of being baptized, being enlightened, being made sons and daughters, being completed, and being made divine, a growth definitely connected to the baptismal reality. That all the power of the divine adoption is invested in the Christian at the moment of Baptism is undisputed, yet our God acts in history in terms of the creation. We learn, change, and become only within the structures of our humanness and never outside of them. So, although the divine potential is vested in the Christian, it is by free choices and progressive awakenings that the woman or man comes to be "one form and one relationship" with Jesus Christ—an insight of John Chrysostom in his *Baptismal Instructions.*

Another early text, *The Rule of the Master,* speaks of the baggage which, in our ignorance, we drag on our journey through the world and from which our baptisms relieve us. We can interpret the passage to mean getting rid of our baggage totally the moment the sacrament is celebrated or we can acknowledge that the laying down of unnecessary baggage is a lifetime task and that it is precisely our baptismal commitment which enables us to lay down the baggage of obtuseness, neglect, and sin in order that we may walk freely into the living waters.

Some Christian prayers of the second century called *The Odes of Solomon* contain a magnificent baptismal prayer here paraphrased: "I have put on the Lord's own life; I stand with his other members. Because I love the Son, I have become daughter and son. Because I delight in the Living One, I become alive."

These passages can be interpreted at a pious distance which enables us to keep the implications of the language at arm's length. We can soar around the heavens ruminating placidly and fail to realize that religious words must be brought to bear on each choice, each relationship, and each event. In *The Pagan Servitude of the Church,* Martin Luther tells us that every day we die and every day we rise. He shared with his predecessors the understanding that baptism placed one forever into connection with the mystery of the death and resurrection of Jesus not in some far off, ethereal way, but in the nuts and bolts of every day.

It is always so much easier to reserve religion to a few flickering vigil lights, an occasional prayer, a chance visit to a wayside shrine or the programmed responses of the Sunday Mass. We have had to remove it from each day lest it require of us more than we are prepared to relinquish. Our spiritual ancestors understood that we must grow into the mystery of the Christian life, a life that imputes redemptive significance to getting up, working, trying to love, going to sleep, and starting off again.

The Adult Rite of Baptism demands of the catechumen that in the context of the community of believers, they prepare to enter this mystery of Jesus which for all the future will make demands upon their lives. The catechumenate is not the time to learn the facts about the Catholic faith, though this intellectual pursuit is not omitted, nor is it the beginning step of entry into the church. It is the acknowledgement of mystery and the acceptance of it—that mystery of faith in Jesus Christ in his death and life as all of this is intrinsically connected to our own lives. Faith is an immense summons which will ultimately ask everything of me.

Baptism pertains to our daily dyings and risings because it is the sacrament that initiates us irrevocably into the mystery of the Christian life. We badly distrust the daily absurd situations and relationships; we become angry and end up wallowing in guilt. The dying experiences of each day cause aspects of our personality to emerge which we have unconsciously repressed—hatred, rage, anger, jealousy, rigidity, fear or terror. As the murky layers of our psyche reveal themselves to our consciousness, faith informs us with the knowledge that this psychic unfolding is already redeemed, touched, surrounded and enveloped in grace. We call out timidly: "I do believe, Lord. Help my unbelief!"

Not only are these experiences redeemed, they are also redemptive. In some mysterious way, because the Body is connected one part to another, what hapens to us has some bearing on all other persons. Our life is redemptive not just in the good and happy parts of it but primarily in the dying moments when the stamina of our humanness is tested against the powers of evil ranged within and outside us. Historically we have used the symbols of warfare to explain our battles with personal pretense and with the cumulative power of all the world's deceit. Though the symbols may be out of fashion to explain some truths, they surely pertain to our sense of struggle with the absurd.

To believe what is written here demands a faith that perceives in the experiences of growth and change those instances which have brought us to maturation and to gradual identification with Jesus. When we do make some faith assessments of our lives, we marvel that the provident God reaches out to save in circumstances so ordinary that most of the time we miss the advents of God completely. Only in hindsight are we able to appraise what has been happening to us. Somehow then we know that baptism is far broader than merely an initiatory sacrament; it has infused all the dyings and risings of each day with redemptive possibilities.

We renew our baptismal promises on Holy Saturday but we might recall the mystery more often with a community of faithful persons. We renounce Satan and all his works and pomps. Perhaps more realistic than imaging Satan as a web-footed, scaley evil-doer, we might ponder whether what we are really renouncing are the temptations to be disgusted with ourselves and all the non-choices which kept us in the limbo of floating on the surface rather than ever living life to the full. We must renounce our own rejections of ourselves, our self-hatred, and all our resistances to becoming free. We renounce being less than what God has created us to be and all the powers that tie our lives up in knots.

Yet, as is true with any religious language or experience, we can stand there and renounce until we are blue in the face without realistically grappling with how "pomps and works" prevent our living the mystery of the life of Jesus holistically. We return home sheltering ourselves once again from the counseling or direction which might alter our usual patterns. We cling to our self-hatred lest, if it go, there should be nothing left of who and what we are. One wonders whether we really believe that Jesus has redeemed every aspect of our lives or whether resurrection signs to us in any meaningful way that we are transformed out of every dying experience. The powers of darkness within us and outside of us have already been vanquished by the power of Jesus Christ and we have been set free. With God's grace and our own efforts to say "yes," we can finally let go of the last shreds of the defense mechanisms, the dreads, the fears, the pains, and the closedness which have tied up our minds. Jesus has redeemed all those areas in us of which we are ashamed and which we feel are unredeemed. Whatever issues from the ambiguity and indefinability which lie at the center of our being is redeemed before we are even conscious of its presence in our lives.

To believe this is to make a faith statement about the

ultimate importance of our baptisms. We have been baptized into the death of Jesus so that we could live the life of Jesus every day. We are never apart from this mystery once we have been brought into contact with it by our faith or by the faith of the community (in the case of infant baptism). That we have been sealed indelibly and forever with the mark of Jesus affirms that we are a people in whose existence ups and downs are not meaningless and absurd; the absurd of all of history is intrinsically connected with and absorbed into the death and life of Jesus.

If we reflect on what is being said here at all, the final statement on the contemplative experience of Jesus is that the meaning of Jesus for the Christian does not imply a life of placid pieties about Jesus but the incarnation of the mind and attitudes of Jesus in us until identification occurs. That which was begun in us in our baptism has reached its climax: humanity and divinity (nature and grace) have once again interpenetrated our lives and it shows in our actions. Yes, we fail, and yes, we make tragic errors of judgment; but through it all the powerful grace of God transforms. We need only become more aware. Our experience of Jesus is not a gentle blend of comfortable feelings and poetic words. There is to be only one eventuality: We must become Jesus in our world.

When faith and life coincide, we recognize the contemplative. Our lives and the life of Jesus are one; both front the absurd within us and in society and both are redemptively significant. This is our faith. We can live no other way. The icon of Jesus is imprinted radically and forever upon our being.

CHAPTER FOUR

The Experience of Faith

"I believe in Jesus Christ and in the salvific power of his life, death and resurrection." This basic assertion is the cornerstone of the Christian life; the creeds of Catholicism, one of which we recite each Sunday, express all the interconnected truths. The faith of Catholics is deep-seated, often inarticulate, but certainly at the bedrock of our self-definition. Yet we find ourselves presently in a period of our spiritual history when an evolution is taking place in our definition of faith. Almost out of our recollection is the memory that faith connoted the gifted ability to believe a series of credal statements; now, we are grappling with the realization that faith requires the internalizing of the creed and its resonance in daily life. We are to follow Jesus by incarnating his life within our own, not by displaying prowess in enouncing for others what we believe.

The evolution is occurring steadily but slowly; we can't change as rapidly as the prophets can name and interpret the current movements of the Spirit. The provident God does not tolerate a triumphal posture and leads us as a people to a wilderness of doubt and questioning as well as to a place of new growth. We have had to scrutinize ourselves and our faith statements to ask whether we truly represent the dispensation of Jesus in our era. Whatever smacks of infidelity and idolatry

must go. To ponder what is taking place in our signi-
fication of faith is to learn that it is not we who are
innovating a theology but to admit that the Lord with
great love is compelling us to a transition time.

Some will argue that in our efforts at ecumenical
sociability we have abandoned our heritage to those
who have consistently preached that it is faith in Jesus
that saves. Many will assess the evolution in the meaning of faith variously as loss or gain, yet we can measure
the value of the evolving most accurately by whether we
find in ourselves a growing commitment to proclaim the
reign of God and to heal the afflicted. An authentic and
genuine faith calls us to read the signs of the times, that
is to give vigilant attention to persons or events that
speak to us of the presence and activity of Jesus in our
times. From this perception of his presence we are then
called to particular choices.

As the evolution is taking place, we should study our
doctrinal heritage with great care. It is imperative that
faith continually seek understanding of itself, a work
traditionally understood as the task of theology. The
Church possesses a vast array of self-understandings
which are not set aside by ingenuous passions for varia-
tion. Through the centuries our theoretical explanations
about ourselves and about God's mighty gesture of
covenant with us have filled many books and have been
the basis for thoughtful and often polemical disputa-
tions. When doctrine becomes, however, the single and
major focus for a religious group, and faith is defined
as a God-given virtue that enables belief in the doctrine,
that group stands in definite need of a reform and a
renewal which would return them to the clarity of the
original dispensation. Catholics have had to move back

beyond the accumulations of centuries of dialogue and speculation, however valuable, to the original message of Jesus.

We had always been fairly secure about how well we could explain our faith. Only recently we've inchoately sensed that a catechism of our creeds was never meant to answer all of life's complex religious questions. In the enclave of the Church, the answers had seemed good to us and had given us a way to interpret ourselves to ourselves and to interested outsiders. When we admitted that some of our answers did not measure the breadth of the questions, we retreated into an embarrassed silence and a sort of intellectual know-nothingism. We are coming to center; faith demands a good amount of rational content. Catholics can be proud of the many saints and scholars who searched after the face of God and spent years carving out the words which articulated their visions.

The ministry of transmitting the wisdom of the past to the present faith community is an important one for a religious group. Some in a religious community have to ponder the wisdom heritage and to distill from it anything and everything that explains the present. To do this it is necessary to have a keen sense of the similarity of the human quest for the divine in all centuries. The task of transmission necessitates an accurate knowledge of texts, a grasp of the process through which a human must move on the path to God and, finally, the ability to speak again the earlier visions in terms comprehensible to the present.

We need to reclaim our classics in their truth and wisdom without cluttering their message with a rhetoric which addressed prior sociological and cultural situations. In order to ponder the alienation and hatred which hell signifies, one need not smell the sulphur fumes or feel smoke in one's eyes as Ignatius suggests in *The Spiritual Exercises*. Yet in contrast with the spiritualities which lead adherents to dissociate body and spirit, Ignatius' skill in employing senses, feelings, imagination and mind in the movement to God shows him to be a wise man indeed. He had an exquisitely accurate faculty of perception into the psycho-physiological and spiritual processes necessary to lead a retreatant through the total panorama of salvation history to the final wisdom of love. Ignatius is a spiritual master not to be dismissed because we too precipitously presume that the images of the sixteenth century do not address present spiritual experience.

Teresa of Avila reveals a wonderfully relevant knowledge of this lifetime progress to God in *The Interior Castle*. We don't live in castles nor are the snakes and vipers which will overrun the castle of the sluggish particularly the symbols we would choose to describe the internal forces of evil which we tolerate and which continually threaten our spiritual maturity. But we avow without question the accuracy with which she outlines the human stages of development in which the grace of God is profoundly at work. Here again is a spiritual master, a woman of marvelous insight into the labyrinthine ways of the human psyche as it is brought to encounter the living God.

Chinese people credit Confucius with being a transmitter of the ancient insights more than with his abilities as an original thinker. The Christian community will always need those who transmit wisdom into current terms and those who reconnoiter new visions.

These are not dissimilar services and contribute equally to the growth of the faith community. The ministry of transmitting wisdom must continue to restore the sapience of the centuries, to select what must not be lost and to insert our heritage into our present explorations into God.

Without serious thinking and reading one is bereft of any creative insights or ideas in the journey of faith. We have matured in many disciplines and no longer need children's mechanisms for explaining mathematical or scientific principles, but too many persons, for some sad reasons, have confined the accumulation of all the religious knowledge they presumed they would ever need to know into a matchbox saved from childhood. After the adolescent forays into atheism, they felt they had exhausted the possibilities of the faith and if they were to live in the real world, they needed to forget the old truths. The credal statements and the daily struggles seemed not to be mutually enlightening.

The electronic church supplants any intellectual content of faith with a speciously comforting palaver. It is pathetic to see intelligent persons accept a fundamentalist interpretation of scripture and a banal if enthusiastic choice for Jesus which nicely manages to exclude the necessity of those daily decisions which mark the serious believer. It is equally disconcerting to see middle-aged and elders in the Church blissfully unaware of the breadth of its tradition as well as of its impact upon the present. These are they who blithely discuss and dismiss the weightiest questions with the most limited cognitive resources. There will never be an adequate substitute for a faith that agonizingly continues to seek understanding of itself so that it can present an alternative to meaninglessness. Our times demand a faith which has the creativity and the maturity to speak its vision into darkness and anguish.

Continual reading to inform faith is what makes a distinction between shallow persons and those whose lives of faith grow always richer. It is not that daily experiences do not speak of God, but we need some interpretation of the daily from the writings of those who, like us, were and are concerned about the nature of faith in ambiguous and complex human situations. Some consistent diet of solid reading is an absolute necessity to anyone who seeks Christian maturity. God is never exhausted, so our minds can never fully grasp the complete mystery of the Godhead and its presence in the economy of salvation. We probably need to chain our leg to a chair once in a while, shut off the TV, and take a crack at some really demanding reading so that we will never forget the earnest and unending seeking which prods faith into decision. Too often what we name doubt or spiritual darkness is nothing other than human dullness and apathy which we have the gall to grace with spiritual names. If there is nothing in the mind, our prayers and our thought will be obviously superficial. True faith crisis is a serious business which most of us do not even approach because what is wrong with our faith is not that it is in jeopardy of being lost but that it atrophies from lack of depth, possibility of growth, or any conflictual situation in which it could be tested and become strong. A minimal and puerile faith cannot bear the burden of presently tangled human issues.

Christians need to challenge society; thus our explanations of faith must be subjected to careful inquiry into their pertinence. The seriousness of our theological effort depends upon the authenticity of the faith which seeks understanding. The contemplative is not seeking an easy lot. No, we search our heritage rigorously, probing the faith it represents, researching the insights which shaped Christian life, and asking the questions of it which so rich a heritage can bear. From this accumulated wisdom, we think and write our own explanations of the present and the suggestions for the future which we help create. This whole process is the ministry of transmission; it is not a task to be taken lightly. It is a ministry necessary in the evolution of our definition of faith. It is a ministry capable of sustaining the energies demanded for those choices and decisions which lead us to radical discipleship.

The evolution in the definition of faith is most notably evident in our sacramental piety. Despite our best efforts to ignore what we want to term "the changes," the Spirit of God has driven us more deeply into the mystery of what it means to live a Christian life. Only if Jesus and his message constitute the center of our life of faith do we have any true sense of sacrament. The restoration of the fundamental significance of the sacraments, in order that each effectively sign its graced reality, is in progress. Cultic celebration and the daily life it expresses are to be brought into correspondence.

The Eucharistic liturgy especially reflects the change in our understanding of faith. We had prayed quietly at Mass and used this time once a week to get in touch with God; it was a serious, spiritual experience for many Catholics. After the decade of the 60's, we felt that this moment of respite from the week's chores was taken from us and a good amount of activity replaced what had been our only space for meditation. What we didn't understand, of course, was that Mass time and meditation time were two different prayer postures; the former, a communal celebration—although inclusive of quiet moments; the latter, a very necessary form of personal centering.

In the last fifteen years we've become used to changes, at least those in the Eucharistic celebration. We have learned that the liturgy is something that we do, not something we watch. The contemplatives among us have found faith deepening in ways that we've only recently found words to express. We come to Eucharist to do here what Jesus asked us to do—to celebrate in symbol what we painstakingly try to live. We have begun to realize that when life and cult are separate, we eat unworthily, we do not recognize the Body, and we are responsible for the death of the Lord. Translated into nonscriptural terms, this language points up the fact that each day we are asked to recognize the Body of Christ in specific works of justice and charity. A refusal to stand counter to opinions and forces which hinder the advance of the kingdom is to fail to recognize the extensions of the mystery of Jesus Christ and thus to be responsible for death-dealing. The Christian whose cooperation keeps people afflicted and oppressed is guilty both of the death of the Lord and the deaths of our sisters and brothers who give their lives that justice prevail.

This seems quite a lot to be in touch with during an hour's celebration once a week, yet it is the mystery of faith which is taking root in the consciousness of the contemplative person. We do not have to be on a religious high during every liturgy, but deep within, the realization of the unity of the Body of Christ must sear our complacencies. We pledge our lives united with the death of Jesus in order that we be transformed into a bread that is ready to be broken. The mystery of passage, ours and the Lord's, is re-enacted whether the liturgy is celebrated well or not, whether the homily is apt or the music good, whether the participants seem to know what they're about or not, even though we long for celebrations where all the external signs are excellent.

When we can blame someone else for whatever is amiss in the parish, we feel we have no personal responsibility to work to change the structures. The other parishioners, the pastor, or the changes themselves have befuddled what should be clear and without flaw. A current author hypothesizes about the extraordinary situation in which the world would find itself if all persons really took responsibility for their lives and stopped blaming husband or wife, priest, bishop or pope, the lady next door, a third grade teacher or one's parents for the way things have turned out. We are tired of carping about the monsignor or the choir; life is too short to spend it railing at human frailty and failure. We want to enter deeply into the mystery of the life of Jesus as it is re-presented in our own. Perhaps we make a choice to seek a different parish. Sometimes we do not attend church. Often we wonder whether we are losing our wits when we still opt to live a Catholic, faith-filled life. If our local religious structures support our desire, we realize we are blessed. When these only thwart our hopes, we struggle to hold to that faith which grasps the mystery of Jesus Christ even within the difficult and painful circumstances of a particular parochial situation.

Most of the time we are present at Eucharist with a faith which testifies that we really do know what we're doing. Beneath any distractions is the confidence that we are carrying out what the Lord commanded. We are trying to sign, in sacrament, the fact that we take seriously and concretely the mandate to love both those near us and all our world neighbors. Monetary donations do not relieve us of the obligation of personal love. We somehow recognize that to celebrate liturgy without any measure of a practical life of love is to celebrate unworthily indeed.

A contemplative approaches worship with an overwhelming sense of the breadth of the Eucharistic mystery. It is at once the celebration of a sacred meal, the redemptive presence of Jesus Christ in our midst and the theandric act which brings about unity, charity and justice in the individual, the Church and the world. It is the central mystery of Christianity and the contemplative is aware of this intensely yet quietly. Long absent is any sense of having to attend Mass under pain of sin. To express in cultic liturgy what is lived in life has become the primary prayer experience. This does not indicate that the contemplative is rapt with attention during Mass. We forget to listen to the readings and find some homilies pointless, or the congregation sluggish, but, nonetheless, we are fundamentally connected to the mystery of the death and resurrection of Jesus as it is celebrated in liturgy and as it is lived in life.

Because all life is experienced by a contemplative as interconnected, we know even the sacramental events unified by a faith that detects, beneath any external details, the redeeming activity of Jesus throughout all the centuries of human history. My daily life with its ups and downs, the Mass, and the death and life of Jesus are in fact one mystery. We ponder this over and over in order that our awareness of the awesomeness of what we celebrate becomes ever more consciously evident. The contemplative rejoices in the celebrations in which presider and participants pray with apparent knowledge of the ramification of the mystery and employ those symbols which signify well the reality of Eucharist. We know overwhelming joy when everyone present pledges life and energy to the reign of God and the healing of the afflicted despite personal woundedness or preoccupations. Nevertheless, no matter how poor the celebration, no matter how out of touch the celebration or celebrators, the mystery of faith in what Eucharist signifies lies deep at the center of the heart and mind of the faithful person. Nothing really ever disturbs this faith except the painful knowledge that the meaning of Eucharist can be completely distorted by those whose vested interests it serves to keep life and liturgy separated. The contemplative knows how radically faith is tested in the hunger and thirst for justice, yet Eucharist promises the eventual hope of the unity and charity of the Body despite all evidence to the contrary. Indeed, to celebrate Eucharist worthily demands a faith beyond that of transubstantiation to that of the transformation of a sinful world by the redemptive power of Jesus Christ.

Another sacrament, that of reconciliation, has also summoned us to new dimensions of faith. The word reconciliation has only recently become a part of our vocabulary. Its ideation is scriptural; it connotes the integrating process within oneself as well as the reconciliation of persons one with another in the Church and world communities. Though it is a word of power and beauty, we are not yet comfortable with its implications or its procedures. The recent history of the sacrament of Penance had each of us confessing our sins privately and as obliquely as possible in a darkened box. Though we may not have liked "going to confession" we were at least comfortable with the manner of proceeding. Now we hear of reconciliation rooms, of meeting the priest face to face, and of different ways to speak of our brokenness. The easiest defense against whatever this change is all about has been not to participate. There are many books written about the details of this sacrament; here I wish to examine the faith with which a contemplative approaches the questions of sin, repentance and reconciliation.

For the contemplative the act of seeking the forgiveness of Jesus Christ through the human community represented by the priest is enveloped by a faith gone far beyond the grade school memories of Saturday afternoon confessions before the movies. Then we knew that to be a Catholic one had to go to confession at least once a year to a lawfully ordained priest. It was a precept of the Church. Not to do this would be to place oneself deliberately outside the fold. Our present faith acknowledges that both personal and social sin cause grave repercussions in our world. The contemplative is a person sensitive to the scandal within and outside oneself, and one who has interiorized law rather than become anti-nomian, as some would accuse. Inherent in this person is the truth that has freed. All that is petty, superficial, selfish, unloving, arrogant, impious, lazy, mistrustful, manipulative, infantile, rigid, closed, dishonest—whatever the particular forms—cause sorrow as from somewhere deep in the murky layers of the psyche, the choice of sin emerges to bring grief and harm to oneself and to others. The classic text of mysticism, *The Cloud of Unknowing,* refers to sin as a "lump," which implies that it is not this or that bad act, but rather those calculated and deliberately chosen obstructions which separate us from the truth and identity of the self. When blocked from our personal center, we are at once separated from God and from the neighbor. Only from within our own truth are we able to relate to another. St. Teresa aptly puts it: "It is foolish to think we will enter heaven without entering into ourselves, coming to know ourselves. . . ." Without this movement to interiority there is no possibility for relationship either divine or human; the lump of sin is falsehood, inauthenticity, and consequently, bondage.

We know that sin is integral to humanity. Scripture says that Jesus became sin for us. Personal reflections, experiences, and even psychological examinations point to its presence, yet by the grace and love of God, we have received the sacramental acceptance of the Lord and of the community of friends and believers. A writer of current mythology, Ursula LeGuin, names a darkness which overshadows the hero with his own name. The darkness or lump of sin is not other than who we are, yet faith assures us that Jesus has redeemed even those aspects of it we cannot name. This constant and forgiving acceptance enlightens the darkness and causes what is godly and light within to shape our future choices.

Barbara Doherty

The pain of humanity is that it is this darkness within each of us that causes injustice to prevail. There are war, violence and greed because the cost of reconciliation threatens our facile explanations for maintaining unjust systems, so we turn aside from the task because it requires too much. We would have to give up our illusions and deceits in order to be reconciled, so we have hidden away from ourselves and pretended not to see the issues. We choose to call light darkness. These are the deliberate compromises of the sinner, a side of one's humanity the contemplative knows only too well. Faith pledges, however, the reconciliation promised by God if we seek it with genuine sorrow. The possibility of personal integrity is offered, but is is not accomplished by ontological magic. We have psychological wounds caused through the years. We have defense mechanisms ready to set up against any challenging new persons or information. We have endless rationalizations why the whole event of reconciliation is pointless. Yet God broods over life awaiting our homecomings.

One difficulty which the contemplative must overcome is the lack of correlation between one's insights about reconciliation and the true and false notions which "going to confession" denotes for Catholics. We are indeed "between the times" with respect to this sacrament. We were discontented with reciting our lists of sins weekly or monthly, and being given certain standard admonitions, yet by no means are we, or many of the clergy, comfortable with the new possibilities. Better a darkened box than looking right into the face of another person with our sins. Worse yet, how does one confront with priestly judgment the penitent who tries to name the various darknesses within? The following dialogues would be facetious if they were not actual:

> *Priest:* The sense you have of choosing a superficial life rather than commitment to discipleship is not a sin. Could you name something you have done that is matter for confession?

> *Penitent:* I bought two obscene books.

* * *

> *Penitent:* I told ten lies.

> *Priest:* As an adult person and as a Christian person you should begin to investigate the root cause of this seeming behavior pattern of deceit. Perhaps you could look to some counseling or spiritual direction.

> *Penitent:* I also fought with my wife. I forgot to mention that.

Immense credit must be given to priest and people who undertake the delicate and enigmatic task of reconciliation with faith, integrity, and the rare commodity of some good sense.

Thomists may recall that they studied each sacrament under three aspects: the outward sign (*sacramentum tantum*), that which is both sign and reality (*res et sacramentum*) and the profound, graced reality of the sacrament (*res tanta*). For the Sacrament of Reconciliation the outline would suggest as outward sign that which penitent says and that which priest hears, ponders, and addresses. That which is both outward sign and hidden reality is the sacramental moment in which the graced interchange is taking place. But the profound reality of the sacrament is that reconciliation which takes place within the penitent by God's vast love, powerful forgiveness, and utter acceptance. This hidden activity of grace is interconnected with the totality of the redemptive mission of Jesus.

Given this triadic scheme, one can understand the necessity for the outward sign to convey as clearly as possible the hidden reality of grace. If the outward sign at any period of our history failed to represent accurately the grace of the sacrament, it became necessary to alter the external celebration so that it corresponded as nearly as possible to the reality. Thus, in order that the repentant sinner know in faith the eternal acceptance and forgiveness of the Lord and the community, the rite in itself must sign this. We are blessed when we find persons with whom we can celebrate prayerfully, seriously and yet joyfully. The current changes in the rite of reconciliation have endeavored to bring sign and reality into focus.

The contemplative priest or penitent strives sincerely for a proper celebration while many others simply state that they do not "go" and they haven't "gone" in several years. Though it is not necessary to seek reconciliation with the frequency with which we used to go to confession, the need and desire for reconciliation and the possibilities for prayer and shared faith that are part of this celebration cannot be underestimated. One hopes that the unfortunate misunderstandings historically associated with transition times can be patiently endured by all of us and altered so that the mystery of reconciliation is witnessed sacramentally in its powerful yet hidden reality. Our world and its peoples need and await reconciliation.

The Experience of Faith

General absolution, communal celebrations, private times of reconciliation, or personal confessions to a friend all have relevance here and sacramental theology has directed its research to these questions. The major project which the faithful person must carry out is to bring the religious experience of reconciliation into focus with the sacrament of forgiveness and healing. Though we may have to wait some years for a rite of sacramental reconciliation that truly signifies the powerful mystery of divine and human acceptance, faith still sees beneath even the weak sign the eternal promise of reconciliation of human and divine into one. The contemplative can embrace each healing and reconciling opportunity.

The concept of social sin has been woven into all that has been previously said, but it demands some specific note. The theology of liberation has articulated that sin which does not stem from personal malevolence but is the evil present in social institutions. Family, religious, civic, diocesan, church, political, or economic institutions have certain aspects inherent in their structures which cause oppression and abuse of persons and keep them from true liberty. Wherever and however systemic injustice occurs, we face the fact of social sin. The contemplative knows that it is not enough to deepen awareness of personal sin; the Church has called us to a social consciousness because we are bound one to another. We must seek answers to the world's ills and attempt the changes of the institutionalized systems that foster injustice. The salvation which Jesus promises extends to social sin and empowers his followers with the concern and the initiative to take issue with the powers of evil in manifold ways. We must shed tears in the night at the fact of injustice, yet work in the daylight with unabated vigor to convert the aspects of oppression that are proximate to us.

The contemplative stance toward the world has never been that of the ostrich; thus the contemplative is one primarily in touch with the reality of social sin. Because we are in touch with our own pain and sin, we are most sensitively in touch with the pain and the sin of the world. The contemplative cannot ignore social sin, but recognizes its presence and implications immediately. Yet our call to justice and reconciliation often goes unheeded because so many spend endless psychic energies whining about the varying facets of personal sin. This is a nice trick for throwing off responsibility for our world while wallowing in the guilt of one's sins, particularly any sexual aberrations. Others set up nest-eggs of varying sorts while the institutions in which they live and in which their monies and time are invested stand as powerful forces against basic justice. The lack of communal celebrations of the sacrament or the ability for a legitimized general absolution allows a further insensitivity to social sin. We are so prone to view reconciliation as only a matter between priest and penitant that we can ignore the social dimension of sin and forgiveness. Communal celebrations of reconciliation could enable the Christian community to face our times ever more realistically.

Scholastics said well that the act of prudence precedes the act of justice. So complex are the social evils which confront us that to unravel the issues and determine the courses of action consume immense energies and cause all but the contemplatives to abandon the enterprise. We can truly be about the work of social change because we have, by God's grace, begun the task of personal reconciliation. Others may picket, research, march, or argue, but when the contemplative fights for human rights, we do so with a commitment that doesn't flag when the newness and the thrill of involvement wear thin. We have watched erstwhile revolutionaries drift away in a new zeal for capital gain and seek lifestyles in which they completely abandoned the quest for human rights.

Not so the contemplative. Though despair dogs our steps and exhaustion and discouragement are ever present, the fire of the word within stokes the energies to jump into the breach again and again. We are called simpletons by the powerful of the world or naive Davids for so confronting the mighty institutional Goliaths. We bear the burden of our own sin as we dare to look squarely in the face of social sin. We call ourselves into question again and again as fools. Psalm 88 speaks our feelings: "I have bourne your terrors with a troubled mind." Yet the fact remains: it will be only the contemplatives who will consistently be about the work of justice. The power which urges forward is not our own. The life of faith is serious business indeed.

Personal sin and social sin are not separate realities. The tangled webs of the former create the situations for the latter. The contemplative prays for personal conversion and for the same within social institutions. The definition of faith broadens to assert that the power of God brings reconciliation even within institutions through the instrumentality of those who hear the cry for justice. Plato's idea of justice as that which brings into harmony one person instead of many suggests a connection between the nature of reconciliation and the work of justice. Faith beholds the redemptive possibility in the sacramental ceremony which can critique our lives and challenge to discipleship those who hear the call in the reconciled silence of personal integrity.

Healing is yet another word new to our faith vocabulary. We frequently associated it with the actions of those who, having learned the psychosomatic origins of many ills, capitalized on the credulity of simple people. Though Catholics have always prayed to specific saints for miracles and healings, even for lost articles and husbands, these requests were not usually seen as connected with Jesus and his healing mission. Often we had appealed directly to the intercession of the holy women and men whose concern for us seemed somewhat closer at hand than that of the Lord. With a bit of embarrassment some now have turned away from this devotion to the saints which modernity has seemingly judged pietistic or credulous. Yet Jesus certainly gave a mandate for healing; he taught that it is an activity which particularly announces the manifestations of the kingdom of God.

Yet the ministry of healing feels foreign and peculiar to us and any gesture toward it seems studied and self-conscious. Against these feelings, we must train ourselves to pray quietly and sincerely for healing. When in the presence of pain, physical or mental, we can call upon the Spirit of Jesus with open hands: "Lord, heal me. Heal this person who is facing so much trouble. Heal the pain and the confusion in this situation." We presume God's love is greater always than our own. We expect no throwing away of crutches, but faith reveals that our concern is heard. God's healing is continuous;

we are simply touching its salvific presence in our hours of need.

With trusted friends and family we might try praying for healing when we are in times that overwhelm or grieve us. We seek no magic solutions to life's complications, but we entrust ourselves to God with an acknowledgement of power beyond our own. When we visit the sick or the elderly, without being intrusive, we might pray for healing instead of bringing useless gifts or chattering endlessly. We must also recognize the faith ministry of those who are weak to those who are well and strong. A gentle sensitivity is imperative. We may not barge into sick rooms, unwanted and uninvited, only to annoy and aggravate people with foolish religiosity. The power of Jesus' healing is shared with invitation; resistance and inauthenticity prevent the divine activity. Healing presumes faith; it does not cause it. The contemplative has a deep, convicted sense of the power of healing which has nothing to do with any furtive glances toward the miraculous. The miraculous is a part of every day for those who can see.

We've had to change our minds about what as children we mistakenly called "extry munction." Our ministers have urged us to seek the Sacrament of the Sick for ills of mind and body. Through this sacrament the healing of Jesus is again extended to the believer in need of the ministration of healing.

Healing prayer should be extended to the reality of social sin as well. The constant eruptions of violence and oppression obviously call for a power for healing beyond our own competencies. Prayer for healing does not take the place of the act of justice, but it is essential to its fruition. Often this healing is evident as the prophet for justice finds the courage to continue. Thus through all times and in many ways, the community of the faithful re-present the healing of Jesus.

Our understanding of faith is changing as well through the numbers of persons who are gathering in small groups to exchange and express faith in order to find a common strength for the spiritual journey. Many are realizing the need and importance of sharing our prayer lives. We had accustomed ourselves to formal prayers at liturgies, rosary, benediction or Vespers, but we are presently experiencing the beauty of self-revelation in sharing prayer with those who struggle through life with us.

It is unfortunate that there is often such difficulty in finding a small community with whom to pray. Many persons are only secure with more formal prayers and feel unable to any great extent to share the depth and intimacy of personal feelings. Some priests, brothers and sisters are content to mutter their prayers in enclosed chapels to which outsiders feel they have no entry. Some people no doubt are unconsciously nervous that the shallowness of their lives might become known to themselves or to others if asked to share faith and prayer. But the processes of renewal are bringing a wonderful renaissance to the churches as we admit and share our individual gifts in a group who come together to seek a fuller and richer faith.

Granted there are always peculiar types whose emotional needs force them to search any and all collectivities for relationship but usually we are edified by the faith and strength of purpose in the communities gathered for faith-sharing. The contemplative shares prayer with various groups who know that the times necessitate believers coming together to witness faith. Corporate pilgrimage presumes sharing visions and a communal charting of horizons. Each pilgrim has personal insights and only in communicating these can we be certain that our common journey is consistently toward God. Sharing prayer creates an attitude of consolidation and strength amid the flux and movement of social changes.

If we're praying with a group for the first or only time, we can expect that since we know each other only very little, the level of our sharing will be limited. But if we pray with the same group frequently it is imperative that there be growth, challenge and a continuing dynamism among the members. Two suggestions are helpful: there is a definite need for intellectual input and development. By processes of reflection and serious discursive thought, the group must deepen its understanding of God. We need a keen sense that we run ever more deeply into the simple yet inexhaustible mystery which God is. To sharpen our awareness, we must bring forward things that we have read or that someone shared with us. The ministry of the transmission of wisdom is important to groups who pray together.

A second suggestion is a plea for a growing and simple openness in order to share visions and insights small and large. We must share pain and joy and share ourselves most of all, truly, authentically and sinfully as we stand before God. We must share and name the processes by which our lives are becoming identified with Jesus.

There are many methods of sharing prayer and these can be varied by the creativity of the group or by occa-

sional outside direction. In our prayer we must be free
to share either a narrative statement, our prayers, or
our feelings which arise from silence, awe, wonder,
praise and of course, from weakness and consternation.
Sharing prayer is not group discussion. We have come
together in faith from our various life situations. It is all
these we bring before the Lord. In our struggles and our
joys measured against the gospel of Jesus, we speak to
one another of a faith that permeates the entirety to
reality. Through the ups and downs communally shared
we are enabled to make new decisions about ourselves
and our directions. Faith has become so much more for
us than an occasional burst of fervoured commitment
during a Eucharistic Congress or a papal visit viewed
from the grandstands.

The change in our definition of faith manifests itself
in yet another way which sometimes surprises us with its
depth. We have often had to stand at the side of human
sorrow—death, separation, miscommunication, or terrible confusions—and we know as we stand there silently holding a bowl of potato salad or a tuna casserole
we have brought, that we stand next to God's revealing
power and presence within the negative aspects of history. When theologians tell about the unutterable God
present immanently within our days we have an overwhelming experience that in sorrow God is mysteriously
most accesible. We have often been present, wordless
and hurting, in these moments of pain, with the transcendent, indeed transcendent, and so unutterable that
the attribute of incomprehensibility is one we know
only too vividly. Yet in this seeming absence we know
presence. We know God present, not conceptually, but
experientially, with some profound sense that life is not

ultimately absurd but rich with redemptive meaning, though we do not feel this nor can we explain it very well.

Recall the times spent waiting in hospital corridors, or standing beside agonizing persons, or having them standing next to you in your suffering. We know somehow obscurely in these moments that life is far more than a multiplication of highpoints. We have not deliberately chosen to substitute sorrow for joy, but in sorrow we recognized God's revelation in the suffering persons as well as in those who stood by without speech, who brought food, or shared clothing. God is present in absence. The word "unutterable" clarifies the nature of God's presence in these pain-filled moments in which there are no words of explanation. Only the very foolish or self-conscious make God-speeches at these sacred and silent times. The revelation of God now is wordless and unutterable. God's transcendence is tangible only to faith; there is neither vision nor word that is revelatory. Silence is the language of contemplation.

A sister or brother is choked with pain, rage or bitterness, yet there is a godliness which manifests itself in the offering of potato salad. We casually write it off saying there was nothing else we could do. The casserole is the external symbol for feelings too ambiguous and difficult to speak. Yet beneath the exchange is the deliberate choice for good, the gesture of concrete love instead of neglect, and the decision of the heart represented by the potato salad.

Religious experience is very ordinary. Surely the saints had more extraordinary things than casseroles to record. No, only the eyes of faith have ever been able to perceive the subtle yet powerful advent of God. Movements to reach out of selfishness to touch the other, to stand present, are manifestations of God within life. Poorly written hagiography made false divisions between sacred and secular and we have been conditioned to believe, when we think about it at all, that God acts only in chapels and monasteries, among monks and nuns, at prayer, in church on Sunday and holydays, but has little to do with the ordinary—especially the ordinary which is filled with pain.

The evolution of our definition of faith is beginning to tell us differently, but we must reorient old pieties as we attempt a catholic stance appropriate to our times. In all the ways examined, our faith is moving toward interiority and away from a sense that we are members in an important, worldwide, religious club. We hear anew the demands of Jesus in very radical ways. In contrast to our old life in the enclave, the present pilgrimage is often frightening. It felt so good to be secure back then; now we find that we have so many personal decisions to make and more than that, we are responsible for them. No one else will pick up the tab for our lives though many in the community of believers will be there to help. When we ponder the evolution that is occurring in our faith, I think most of us are glad. Jesus' summons should never have become humdrum. It must cost us something—we who have been baptized into the mystery of his death so that we might live a life of radical discipleship.

CHAPTER FIVE

The Experience of Discipleship

BY the grace of the Holy Spirit there is something new happening among us. If we listen to ourselves, we might discover a different rhetoric with which we are trying to explain our lives. In the last few years, we have over-worked the language of self-fulfillment along with the rest of our country: "Become assertive. Overcome guilt. Say no. Don't be afraid to be yourself. Trust yourself. You're number one." The language of the 70's evidenced our national posture of self-actualization. In the battle against a low self-esteem, the personal consciousness movement offered us a plausibility structure for healthy doses of belief in ourselves. We learned that it was legitimate to pay attention to our own needs and to move away from a neurotic subservience to the whole world.

Now we are asking: Is this all there is? We suspect that the reality of Christianity is definitely not measured or encompassed by the rhetoric of self-fulfillment; we are listening anew to the summons to self-denial: "Deny yourself. Pick up your cross. Follow me. Do what I have done before you." The words resonate with a welcome relief from studied efforts at self-definition. An invitation to sacrificial love and commitment to discipleship offers us something vast enough to which to pledge our lives. We feel that the rhetoric of self-denial is not a souvenir from asectical manuals but calls to what is best and deepest in us. To set boundaries to our native instincts for limitless frontiers, to desire simpler ways to live, and to search for adequate explanations of our times are the tasks we accept as we recall the truth of Jesus' message for self-transcendence.

Our present spirituality, that is, the way each of us tries to come to God, has been formed by a biblical theology. Although we are largely unaware of the historical processes which created it, we have a religious language capable of naming and interpreting our ordinary experiences as somehow revelatory of the divine. Whatever the quality of the exhortations to discipleship in the various parochial contexts, by some mysterious providence we have arrived corporately at a challenging time in the saga of the following of Jesus. The renewal called for by the faithful and summed up in conciliar documents is reaching its starting point. The groundwork has been laid for that kind of internal change which confronts our shallow excuses for the separation between faith and life.

Our current dichotomies are not those between liberal or conservative, ordained or lay, progressive or traditionalist, but that between discipleship or comfort. We have acculturated discipleship to such a degree that religion has become part of the formula for leading a socially acceptable neighborhood life. The gospel, however, stands as silent yet powerful critic to a tamed and moderate religion.

"Go sell what you have, give to the poor, come follow me."

"He bound up his wounds, took him to an inn, and said he would stop on his return trip to see how the injured man was."

The Experience of Discipleship

"Lord, when did we see you hungry, or thirsty, or in prison, or naked?"

We are discovering the implications of discipleship, although conflictual situations occur between what some in the Catholic community hear as the summons of the Lord and what others regard as the overthrow of all they have held as religiously intact. Often we can identify in ourselves a love-hate relationship to the institutional aspects of religion, as well as growing tensions between the following of Jesus and the organizational trappings of a respectable religion. We are not revolutionaries nor querulous criticizers of authority, but we sense ourselves called to a life of discipleship which is then expressed in liturgy, whereas the ordinary sacramental piety unconnected with life makes absolutely no sense to us. What is the Spirit asking of the Church? What does the Lord Jesus intend for his followers?

Jesus preached the kingdom of God. Wherever and whenever the blind began to see, the deaf hear, the lame walk, or the poor hear the gospel—there the kingdom is present. The disciple is not to look to the north, south, east or west in search of the kingdom; it is in our midst when God's reign is proclaimed and when the afflicted experience healing. Repeatedly Jesus asked that we see all of life in this context. When the disciples are sent out, it is with the authority necessary to carry on this mission. The disciples were to leave the cities of those who refused to hear the word of the kingdom and shake the dust from their feet as they left. Stern instructions indeed.

The message of the kingdom has social as well as personal implications: Not only is individual blindness overcome, but the evil and sin in societal relationships is open to the challenge of the kingdom. Into the lives of all people, Jesus brought the message of Yahweh: *You are to be free.* Peace and justice which are God's names are to be yours. Jesus' conflict with those who resisted his message does not give us any reason to presume he was talking about a kingdom which would come after death and after the general resurrection. Even the most casual reading of the scriptures tells that the reign of God is both a present and a future reality, and that the disciples are intrinsically connected with its occurrence.

Faith believes that God acts despite the limitations of our vision about the whole divine project, but our human experiences force doubt and uncertainty upon us. We live with the painful knowledge that the blind do not see, that captives are not freed, and the poor are often denied the gospel. We cry out of despair because we have no comprehension of how the kingdom can be present either in ourselves or in a society where injustice prevails. We question whether the faith which the follower of Jesus is supposed to have in the presence of the kingdom is simply a meaning structure which a despondent person, unable to make any sense out of our universe, needs to impose on life and time. Perhaps we are afraid that if we do not impute some significance to our history, cynicism and emotional breakup will be the only ways to cope with the ugliness and scandal of a world that dismays us each day with new types of inhumanity.

Jesus preached parables about seeds to give confidence against the doubts his followers experienced. Only faith can see in the smallest mustard seed the power to become a tree. Only a bold and daring faith can go against what is apparent and believe that hidden seeds are being transformed into thirty, sixty, and one hundred bushels of grain. Jesus experienced rejection by neighbors and friends; he felt the pressures of evil gathering against him and conspiring toward his death. We can certainly presume that he had to invoke the power of God for strength in knees that faltered and in arms that grew weary. Humanly, he had to rely on a faith that assured him that the enterprise of God would not fail. The obtuseness of the disciples must have occasioned his greatest sorrow. In addition, it was the poor, the unfortunate, and the downtrodden who listened to Jesus' message while most of the religious people refused his word; this hypocrisy caused anger in Jesus, an anger recorded many times in the scriptures.

We are to preach the kingdom and be an occasion of it, yet the disciple lives continually with the tension of the present and the not yet. We inhabit two worlds—not this present one and then heaven—but rather the City of God and the Human City, to borrow St. Augustine's terms. The Human City is the people in whom injustice and disharmony prevail while the City of God is the people who hunger and thirst for justice and in whose lives faith, hope and love take precedence over greed and deceit. This people cares that the blind are enabled to see and the lame can begin to take a few halting steps.

For Jesus, as well as for his disciples, there is an assurance born of faith, that indeed seeds change into crops. It is a confidence which is not simplistic but one that trusts that life has surprises of love and transformation. Faith in the promise that has been given is entirely different from a self-determined struggle to make sense out of absurdity. Faith looks and finds hidden goodness, change, growth, blindness overcome, and many people who manage an integrity between faith and practice.

The kingdom is definitely God's doing. In the history of the Jewish people, God intervened to lead the Israelites along salvific paths and the covenant offered love and fidelity forever. Our ancestors believed the word of the faithful God. In Jesus and thus in the human, the Christian knows the incarnate presence of the covenant. The fidelity and love of God took mortal flesh in order that we could see with our own eyes what the dispensation of grace would look like. "When you see me, Philip, you see what God is." The reign of God becomes present in Jesus and also in those who listen to the call to discipleship and who follow in faith; thus the kingdom continues in our midst because God continues to be faithful in very ordinary human events. By belief in God's dispensation and by the choices we make to live in particular ways, we give testimony that acknowledges Jesus as the meaning of our lives, his mission as our work, and his death as a possible eventuality for us if we are identified as his followers. As we make each daily choice that is for, rather than against, the advent of the kingdom, we are involved in proclamation and healing. If, however we live uninvolved with the word of God, if all our efforts are directed toward our own prosperity and self-fulfillment, if we have espoused narcissism as a way of life, then self-denial, the cross, the giving of life for another and the self-sacrifice it takes to work against impossible odds for human rights, sound only like so much pious rhetoric.

Unbelief trails our days. One has got to be witless to choose self-denial; it is bad enough that inequitable economic systems impose it upon us. Surely it is more reasonable to lead a normal, decent life than to get caught up in some religious fanaticism that demands so much.

"What does this mean? A completely new teaching in a spirit of authority!"

"To you the mystery of the kingdom of God has been confided."

"They found him too much for them. Jesus' response to all this was: No prophet is without honor except in his native place."

"He began to teach them that the Son of Man had to suffer much, be rejected by the elders, the chief priests and the scribes, be put to death and rise three days later."

"They gave from their surplus wealth, but she gave all she had to live on."

"Because of my name you will be hated by everyone. Nonetheless, the one who holds out till the end is the one who will come through safe."

"My God, my God, why have you forsaken me?"

We have to pray a great deal for the courage of discipleship. It is a way of following Jesus that cuts across all groupings of young or old, gay or straight, male or female, liberal or conservative. All of us are called to be followers in the most radical sense. The meaning of discipleship is that we choose to be connected daily to the mystery of the death of Jesus and to his resurrection. It is not sufficient to celebrate these sacred events in liturgy; they must be repeated in our lives by means of our choices and decisions as faith informs our days.

There is no moderate way to read the gospel and there is no middle road to follow Jesus. The religious madness that gospel language suggests tells us that we really do have to walk the extra mile, which, translated, reads: "Assert yourself in your own deepest truth and at the same time reach out with great love to another." The balance of these polarities seems utterly impossible most of the time, yet the task does not describe the doormat personality. Discipleship requires the process to self-actualization in order to deny the self for the greater good. Transcending ourselves presumes certain skills gained through painful life situations in order to channel powerful emotions into personal strengths. There are gaps between the needs and ignorance deeply ingrained in our psyches and those enlightenment moments and choices to follow Jesus. It is precisely our humanity, just as it is, which is the graced instrument for proclamation and healing.

Each life decision is to be for the kingdom. Any prudential reflection on the meaning of existence must insure that the blind will see. We are sinners—weak, superficial, greedy, thieving, even murderous in our hatreds—yet it is to participation in the redemptive mystery of Jesus that we are called. Faith tells us this is true. A socially acceptable religion demands so little of us. If we share some part of our lives with those who will think and pray about discipleship with us, we can admit gradually the mysterious requirements henceforth laid upon our lives.

There is a lifelong and cylic process involved in our becoming disciples. Long years of discipline occasion our decision to follow Jesus in a more radical manner, but a discipline without that perjorative connotation that makes our stomachs ache from repressed guilts. Discipline is a normal fact of life for a contemplative; it involves responsible decision-making as life batters us with contradictions and conflicts we would not personally choose. In each instance, by the transforming power of God, if we choose life and not death, we gain a new receptivity to Jesus' message and a new readiness for discipleship. For the contemplative, discipline signifies steadfastness; this is one who, though not oblivious to the tensions of each day, waits with patience for the Lord. Waiting is an active stance of thinking, speaking, praying, working, weeping and laughing, and with increasing faith, coming to know that God acts to save in human terms. The mystery of incarnation is at hand not in strange and extraordinary circumstances but right within the normal fabric of uneventful days.

Social psychologists have made us aware of stages through which humans arrive at maturation, wisdom, or self-actualization. Growth in discipleship is no exception to this natural process. A barrier to our gaining a sense that all of life, including religious development, is processive has been a presumption that once "in the church" or once we went along with the rules with some exactitude, there was not much more connected with being a Catholic. Any identification of religious experiences seemed unnecessary for those ontologically saved by the power of sacrament.

A moment happens, however, when, as adults, we meet the Lord and are powerfully attracted to a deeper commitment in faith. An unmistakable summons to discipleship is heard which calls for a response which, if omitted, would concretize us in behavior patterns that controvert the new possibility being revealed in us.

In the initial stage of discipleship, we kind of "hang around" with Jesus; that is, we can't get the whole plaguing matter out of our minds. We read or hear something which adds to the original insight. Certain people, a lecture, or some book adds shape to the experience which begins to be confirmed in us. Usually we are rather easily able, at first, to set the whole affair aside; one need not, after all, get too entangled in all this Jesus business. Yet the summons finds us in whatever corner of our minds or of the earth we try to hide. There is some other dimension to our lives that we must seek out. Everything that has filled our days begins to be not enough to challenge and demand of us. We seek out some parish involvement or some service to the needy in order to placate the summons. There seems to be little specific instruction within us or around us as to how we are to carry out this mysterious challenge which we cannot forget without doing violence to who and what we are. We try to imitate Jesus: We try to be more open to people, to be kinder and receptive, to listen, to help the needy, or to pray more.

This beginning stage of discipleship may last a longer or shorter period of time. There is no time schedule for the Holy Spirit who is at work to carve the icon of Jesus Christ upon our being. One fact is radically present to us: *there is something more.* We do not know how to name what we feel. We may seek the advice of the parish priest who may or may not understand what we are talking about unless he too is listening to the call to a more radical way of following the Lord. We will eventually meet someone who can clarify the interior vision. The East Indian has a marvelous saying about the guru. One does not travel the whole world seeking the holy teacher. When you are ready, the guru comes to you. If we remain steadfast in the original insight, vague as it may seem, someone or something will penetrate our stolidity and begin to clarify what is occurring.

The next stage of the process begins with specific instruction. The teacher speaks about the kingdom of God and how all life is to be understood in this context. We are called upon to take definite steps; it is not enough to ponder the mystery of the kingdom in prayer. We must associate ourselves with those who were given a mission to proclaim the reign of God and to heal the afflicted. We decide to organize into our lives some activity for carrying this out, and we feel a certain surge of joy as we begin to sink our teeth into this new involvement.

The only difficulty is that very soon we learn that ministry for the kingdom is not a matter of folding bandages for mission hospitals, of delivering clothes or food to poor families, but that a change is demanded in the way we think about practically everything. The message of Jesus cuts daring inroads into our minds; the volunteer efforts are worthy but not yet the answer. The demand for radical discipleship presses upon us with even greater urgency. The evaluation of the disciple is quite clear in the gospel:

"Let those who follow pick up the cross each day and deny themselves."

"What does it matter if you gain the whole world but suffer the loss of your own identity?"

Our identity in the midst of a tumultuous world seems insignificant, but Jesus evidently thought differently. If we build great barns, the gospel refers to us as fools. The contest within us is between the banal, which fascinates, and the gospel, which terrifies. Discipleship and everything that is not discipleship are locked in mortal combat. We have heard sermons preached against "Sunday Catholicism," but now the significance of the phrase has awakened in our thoughts. To be Sunday Catholics is now incomprehensible and inapplicable to our lives.

In due season the implications of discipleship become clearer. There is no moment of our time, no relationship, no place or idea that can be excluded from the process. The rigorous human task of interiorization is taking place in us. The permeation of our being by faith does not imply that religion is constantly on our minds or reflected in our speech, but that our lives are now shaped by certain serious convictions and there are no reserved compartments.

We laugh and joke, row boats, and take the kids to the zoo but no activity is outside the following of Jesus which specifies each day. Though we frequently misread the cues, though we are often dense to the demands relationships make on us, though we are slack in listening to the mandates of the Church to justice, the invitation to a contemplative faith has been imprinted on us. Though we may try to refuse, we cannot escape the designation. Why us? Our lives are so ordinary. All the reasons the prophets offered the Lord Yahweh for remaining uninvolved in the history of their time, come to our lips and sound equally puny. "I have called you."

The Experience of Discipleship

A claim has been put on our lives and the cost of discipleship has permeated every facet of who we are.

It bothers us constantly that we find ourselves so shallow. When we should be concerned for the hungry of the world, we hear ourselves complaining that the store does not stock a preferred brand of paper towels, or that the stewardess is exceptionally slow in serving drinks on this flight. Do the complexities of our personality ever come to integration? Wise persons tell us that it is the Lord who saves and integrates, but we can't deny our roots: A "do-it-yourself" attitude pervades even our process in discipleship.

Faith grows the way the seeds grow while the sower sleeps and works at other tasks. We have to resist the desire to pull the carrots up to see if there is hidden growth under the earth. Only with hindsight, when we look back to the moment of the original summons, do we perceive that indeed, we are different. We are loved by a mysterious Other who continually frustrates our immobilities. Our discipleship does not become clearer, only more complex, and we always have more questions than answers. The contemplative learns only very slowly that disintegration is a necessary component of the integration process; brokenness is gradually healed and weakness gently empowered. In ministerial responsibility we are forced up against the conflicts that cause us to change our agenda many times. The Lord might have designed a primrose path to the parousia, but life seems filled so often with anxiety, tragedy and injustice. The contemplative finds answers—which are usually non-answers—in facing life the way Jesus did and in investing life with the same meaning which Jesus gave it.

All of life is to be lived in the context of faith in the present and in the final reign of God, in the healing of afflictions of all kinds and in the disciple's engagement with the divine and hidden activity.

Like Peter, we want to rebuke Jesus when the topic of dying enters the conversation. We favor uncomplicated integration, not the messy, mending-fences-over-the-long-haul kind. We like to greet the Lord in the gentle breeze not in hurricanes, fire or storms:

"Can you drink of the cup?"

"What must I do to gain eternal life?"

"If your hand causes you to sin, cut it off!"

"You will receive the hundred fold and persecution."

"There was a widow who gave everything she had."

The story haunts us with its obvious point: We'll never get away with giving a few dollars here and there. We are summoned to concern and care for our world and its people and called to give all we have. To what? When? Where? Answers focus as the endless procession of people and events alters our mindsets. We are invited from office, kitchen, classroom or factory to broaden our worldview and with critical eye to examine our commitment to the mission of Jesus. Whatever our age or capabilities, our talents are not to be buried in a napkin to be delivered untouched into eternity. Responsibility for our times beckons us.

Discipleship need not mean that we must abandon all we presently embrace, though that might be the eventuality. It is a call to broaden our horizons, to launch out into the deep, and to test our abilities to walk on water. All our relationships must be scrutinized in the light of the gospel. Do we use people because of our own needs, manipulations and schemes? Who are the blind, the deaf, the lame? Where are the poor? How is it that we must preach the gospel? "Lord, we are too young. We stutter. Send our sisters or brothers. Lord, here we are. Send us." The ambivalence of our dedications and our refusals mock our attempts at commitment and courage.

As the sense of discipleship exerts a total hold on our lives, the Jesus whom we met in our initial vision seems now, in yet another stage of the process, to abandon us. Imitation of Jesus seems shallow and inane. We are perhaps nothing but a nostalgic remnant from the high school sodality. What is now occurring is the graced transformation from a disciple who *imitates* Jesus to one who, as contemplative, *identifies* with Jesus. To follow Jesus we have to go beyond doing nice deeds that mirror the activity of Jesus. We must die. Jesus was crucified as a result of the way he lived his life. He was accused of blasphemy, of speaking of God falsely, and then he was killed. He did not retract any of his teachings. He did not apologize for insulting the religious leaders of his time who quite cavalierly were able to overlook the prophetic significance of his word. Deep within, the realization begins to dawn on the disciple that imitation has to become identification. We must do what Jesus did. We must die many times to all the pretenses and foolishness within ourselves as well as to whatever compromises we have made with the intricate webs of sin and injustice in our church and in society.

We must be vigilant for false Christs, false prophets, and the vanity and uselessness of paths that lead nowhere. Fidelity and steadfastness are imperative at this final stage of discipleship. The temptation to turn back is overwhelming—back to cynicism, back to lollygagging through our lives or back to a tamed religious practice. The mission of healing and proclamation is ours to be carried out, yet sometimes at this juncture even those who love us call us to return to sanity. Why this venture into territory so unfamiliar to our neighborhood?

"He is out of his mind."

The true disciple is not marked with that exuberant fervor that punctuates each sentence with calling upon the Lord to bless the occasion. This woman or man is anything but a revivalist preacher. The contemplative is pained by the vision most of the time, yet the fire has burned within and cannot be dismissed blithely as if nothing had been seen. The rejection by friends or family is not the pathological kind that is self-inflicted. "Everybody hates us because we love Jesus." No. Never that. The rejection is more like an estrangement because we have gone somewhere that we don't know how to locate for ourselves let alone for anyone else. Those with whom we had previously walked now seem somewhere else, both to us and to themselves. Different comrades rise to join us. We meet fellow travelers who can fathom the dilemmas we are encountering because of their own rich experience of following.

There is an increased sense of vigilance about us. The command to watch and pray has new dimensions. We are not fearfully waiting for the sky to fall, but awaiting the next set of directions which will point out the next step. We do not know from what place, person, or situation these may come. We must stay awake. The Lord may come like a thief in the night. All these exhortations to vigilance now take on new meaning for us. Where, perhaps, we had once heard them from the pulpit as dire warnings against getting caught in some act of impiousness, now they read like pleas against sluggishness and mediocrity. Somehow, crazily, at the center of ourselves, there begins to be felt a new hope and joy, one born of struggle and fidelity. No Pollyannaism ever, but a kind of stillness, a gentle, firm faith, a merriment which makes us laugh and dance, and a definiteness of purpose in the face of agonizing doubts—all lie at the center of our commitment.

Here and there we fail miserably—sometimes we even fail grandly. But what we had been taught about the nature of kingdom as God's doing and not ours begins to become radiantly clear for us. The power that proclaims the reign of God and the power that heals the afflictions of the world is not ours but God's, a power made perfect in our weakness.

A facile reading of this latter sentence makes an outsider infer some praise of incompetence. One can be a fool and perform shabbily, because after all, it is not our work that saves but the Lord's. The disciple ripened, mellowed and chastened by the years knows only too clearly the precise balance between one's own weakness and the power of God. Jesus died and was raised up and transformed by the power of God. An archbishop is assassinated and his life is transformed by the power of God into gospel and bread by which many can eat and live. The disciple must die as well, many times over, and be transformed by the power of God. Only in this consummate identification with Jesus does the reality of discipleship reach its fullest potential.

For the U.S. Catholic, the last word to be said of this process to discipleship is that we do not choose it ourselves and we do not make ourselves into this brand of believing Catholic. It is an occurrence of the kingdom that is God's doing; this blind one has seen. It is this life to which all followers of Jesus are called, a life, not an exception, but the rule. Though many of us have compromised somewhere below 50 percent of what following is all about, nonetheless, the magnitude of the call to discipleship exerts its summons upon us. The call is not just for monks, nuns, and priests but for all followers who bear the name Christian. The following of Jesus penetrates every corner of our lives. When we truly know, deeply and interiorly, that the power of God is made perfect in our weakness, then we have become disciples. The work of mission can now be fruitful because we are not involved in it for prestige or vested interests. We really want the blind to see, including ourselves. We see reality in the context of the kingdom with the eyes of faith. Because of the mystery of incarnation, human time has, for as long as it exists, become salvific. This is why what is ordinary and daily is so very precious.

The one who follows Jesus in the manner of disciple shows yet another aspect of the portrait of the contemplative person. Whether in or out of a monastery, the hallmark of this person's life is integration—integration of all the facets of life dealt with painstakingly—yet within the consciousness of this individual's becoming one. This oneness approximates the unity and simplicity of the Godhead. Religion is not compartmentalized for the contemplative, but faith is interiorized as each decision is made for the kingdom of God. For centuries this radical vision of the unity of reality has typified the contemplative human being. This person before all others is able to work for justice, because this person, as different from all others, possesses a purity about activity; because of this person there are fewer cows at the ends of the ropes. Fragmentation of motive and multiple personal needs and desires have given way to a unity of purpose which fortifies a true disciple against obstacles. This follower has become leader.

CHAPTER SIX

The Experience of Prayer

MANY words have been written and spoken about prayer; people travel far and pay lots of money to learn how to do it better. This latter phenomenon makes one sad, for prayer should be simple, free, and freeing, and that which is becoming ever so gradually what we are rather than what we do or say. Prayer is communion with God; it can be expressed in prayers that we say or expressed in our lives as a quiet sense of being centered in God. Sometimes we are unable to name the center God; it is mystery and power beyond our own. It is still point and ground of who we are. It is meaning and significance. It is presence and absence.

To illustrate the dual expressions of prayer, one can use the Our Father. It is indeed a prayer that we can say, but it must declare a fundamental communion with God in each day or it remains words which are not synchronized with life in any way. "Give us this day our daily bread," or "Forgive us as we forgive others," or "Thy kingdom come," are attitudes which form choices. The words prayed at liturgy or wherever must represent the content of daily praxis. The person who prays always is the one whose basic dispositions and actions each day (no matter what it contains) reflect a deep-seated faith in the revelation of divine with what is human.

Barbara Doherty

Jesuit Bill Callahan has urged us to seek our model for prayer in Jesus. The Gospels record that Jesus prayed a prayer of perspective apart from the crowds on some occasions, yet the biggest percentage of his time was spent in the prayer of presence, a kind of prayer synonymous with contemplation. It denotes that the totality of the person is engaged with the present and the people in it. We recognize the gift of such presence when it is given. Here is someone truly present to us, and someone whose complex of motivation is focused in this moment without preoccupation or tedium. We have all had the experience of feeling invisible to a woman or man who is utterly self-absorbed.

Jesus prayed the prayer of presence in the midst of the multitudes who constantly surrounded his life. However we go about it, the prayer of gaining perspective on life, prayed apart from our daily situations, must result in a growing ability to pray the prayer of presence. The truth of our prayer will be evident in a greater sensitivity to people's needs, a sharpened awareness of the serendipity of creation, and an ever-deepening commitment to justice. If our prayer does not have these multiple effects, we ought to examine the notions we may have about it in order to test its authenticity.

Gaining perspective is a necessary component of human and divine growing. We need to step aside in order to examine our lives, to see who and what we are, and to ask penetrating questions of ourselves and our world, not in order to answer them, but to sharpen their focus. However we go about it, we know an increasing need to gain perspective. We need to know again and again how all of life is inseparable from the happening of the kingdom of God.

The Experience of Prayer

In our prayer of perspective we can accustom ourselves to live in the ambiance of God's reign. Much of our world is a violent one and we know the powerlessness of trying to change it. We want to do what writer John Shea so aptly proposes: Live a life which proclaims an alternative. By gaining perspective we can make determinations about ourselves and choose alternates to greed, power, shallowness, cynicism, complacency, and elitism. We don't do this by browbeating ourselves into good behavior, but by asking God to extend that infinite patience and grace which compels to discipleship.

The prayer of perspective can and does sometimes go off in peculiar directions. Some persons spend good amounts of time at prayer, yet their ordinary appearance conveys only tension, chronic carping, and a lack of any kind of interest, let alone love of anyone else. These are external indicators that much of what is called prayer is merely putting in time and checking off another religious duty. The fruits of the spirit of prayer are not evident. If a woman or man is prayerful, then charity, joy, peace, patience, kindness, endurance, and all the other effects of the Spirit's presence which we memorized as children, should be apparent to the onlooker. Without seeming to criticize foolishly, it is nothing short of dismaying that many lay persons, clerics and religious who have supposedly spent time in prayer through the years should turn out to be such shallow, self-centered, small-minded human beings. Certainly many Our Fathers have been said by them. Why, at least judging externally, have such persons not become what they have said? I do not refer to occasional, even frequent personal failings, weaknesses or moments of irritability; rather, I am trying to assess those lives in which the time of prayer and worship has seemingly failed to result in any greater ability to love. Rigidity and tension do not manifest the Spirit. Prayer should be simple, free, and liberating. It should be becoming what we are more than what we say or do.

From anything one reads about the discernment of spirits, if a person seeks God in truth, then some evidence of the presence of the Spirit should be conspicuous. All self-chosen, self-aggrandizing, and personally dishonest ways of prayer must be set aside. A good friend or spiritual director can lead the honest seeker in the path that God faithfully and strongly is indicating. Each one of us can at least pray for truth in our prayer and beg the Lord that we not be allowed to deceive ourselves. We don't want to die singing: "It's life's illusions I recall; I really don't know life at all. It's love's illusions I recall; I really never knew love at all."

We have to locate space somewhere, both in our heads and geographically where we can pray the prayer of perspective. Some can pray it riding the bus or subway, waiting in line, fishing, golfing, gardening, walking, or sitting in the bathroom. This prayer requires stepping aside from the normal patterns of our lives either on the roof of the house, the basement, or wherever we can for a while gain perspective on our lives. An Indian scripture, the *Śvetāśvatara Upanishad* suggests:

> In a level clean place, free from pebbles, fire and gravel, favorable to thought by the sound of water and other features, not offensive to the eye, in a hidden retreat protected from the wind, let us perform our religious exercises.

A gravel pit or garbage dump won't do, but some small beauty, even a blade of grass springing up from concrete, can get us started. Just as Jesus did in his prayer, we situate our lives in the context of God's life. Ours is not to be a treadmill existence; we are followers of the Lord. What claim does this statement make on our days?

We go about the prayer of perspective in many different ways. A liberty of spirit is imperative. We cannot adopt prayer forms and postures that are unsuitable to the ways in which the Lord is leading us. Prayers that suited us at one time may no longer have any meaning. We must be content with this spiritual mutation and admit that it is the Lord who changes the directions for us. We probably become aware of this dynamic or are able to put words to it only in hindsight.

A contemplative is utterly free in regard to prayer. This person can use whatever methods are helpful and let the rest go. With the altering levels of maturation, different processes will suit who we are becoming. The contemplative is open to the variations, knowing that all of life and thus, obviously, one's prayer life, takes new shapes as the years go along.

We need to put something into our heads to ponder so that when we come to prayer, the content is commensurate with our human maturation. We need to work at some challenging spiritual or theological material every once in awhile or our piety will in fact be merely a facsimile of mature Christian faith.

We may need to spend some time learning a few helpful psychophysiological methods: regulated breathing, postures, exercises, dance and prayer movements, yoga, repetitive meditations, zen, or a prayer of centering. These enable us to move past the "God bless mama, God bless daddy, God bless the dog" prayers of childhood. It is true that although we have changed the words, many of us have retained the basic structures of children's prayers as the most common form of approaching the inexhaustible mystery of God. Jesus has asked us to become like children, in the sense of genuine creativity, openness and enthusiasm but certainly not in the sanctification of naivete or immaturity.

A contemplative frequently prays the prayer of perspective through various forms of meditation. There is a formality about meditation techniques and a teacher may have to direct us in their use. We ought to note, however, many of our own quiet means of integrating are not different in essence from some classic forms of meditation.

One method may be most easily explained as thinking, pondering or reflecting in a serious, discursive fashion. Examples are many:

1.) We frequently think things through about our lives. We do this sincerely and purposively. Where are we going? Why are we doing what we're doing? This is one form of meditation.

2.) We ponder nature in concrete jungles or rural areas. We examine lifegiving and destructive aspects of creation, both of which aid in our reflecting on the meaning of order and disorder in our universe and in ourselves.

3.) We read the Gospels using mind and senses to discern the meaning of Jesus' life and to discover the metaphors in our own which reflect the Word. We mull over the scriptures till the message informs our consciousness.

4.) We find material for pondering in art, music, literature, theatre and movies. All offer deepening insights into life. Through the intuition of the artist, we confirm our humanity estranged from, yet forever assumed by God.

5.) We read various books, magazines, or newspapers which keep us responsibly in touch with world issues. We adopt positions in situations of continual flux and challenge.

6.) During our aging process, we may sometimes ponder our deaths, a kind of meditation advocated by both Buddhists and Christians throughout their spiritual histories. When we do this well and without morbidity, we gain a somber attitude which encourages us to love and to be free, the two qualities with which we must ultimately come before the Lord.

Using non-discursive methods, we might define meditation as a process of "un-thinking." Many have read about or tried various nondiscursive meditation methods such as yoga, zen, or transcendental meditation. Perhaps we know of the prayer of centering. The meditator is advised to repeat a word: God, Peace, Love, or Jesus, using it as a means to keep the mental powers collected. The words summarize the cumulation of faith and thus are particularly significant and powerful in the progress to centering. As we repeat the word, we exclude all other concepts. If we persevere in this discipline, the word is first on the lips, then in the mind, but finally, through days and years of faithful living, we become the prayer which we say. Many have prayed short aspirations, but we are referring here to a specific meditation technique in which the word is repeated while the meditator moves inward on the journey to center. To continue this effort as a prayer method implies a growth away from mere automatic repetition to affective prayer to that silent consistent prayer in life which is contemplation.

In either the discursive or non-discursive meditation methods, one works at the exclusion of multiple mental images. When we meditate discursively, we channel our thought to one subject. Such concentration on the one paradoxically brings about the integration of the many. The deliberate exclusion causes a disposition to inclusiveness. A process of integration is taking place. In non-discursive methods, we exclude any conceptualization at all, working always toward emptiness and stillness. This is not exclusion for exclusion's sake, but the emptying of the faculties so that in this meditative single-mindedness, life becomes clearer and cleaner. We are able to come in touch, at least momentarily, with a unity or oneness of being in which the daily ambiguities find some kind of resolution at least temporarily.

Meditation requires discipline. But doesn't all of life? Somehow we need to look again at what we're talking about when we speak of the discipline of meditation. We know the discipline of running, of exercise, or of a proper diet. Without some reasonably faithful regulation of diet and movement, we use our bodies badly. In the same manner, a life of serious reflection demands discipline. We can scatter our psychic energies here and there, or we can channel our lives with directions and goals which bring us to a heightened awareness of the importance, power and mystery of life itself. In Christian terms, we pray the prayer of perspective so that our lives of discipleship are not careless. We pay attention to persons and events focusing these in the Lord by whatever methods are simple, free, and freeing.

The various techniques of meditation lead easily to prayer in which we speak to God in concern, praise, thanksgiving, affirmation, and love. We listen quietly to the word within as we discern the movements of the Spirit in ourselves during either very brief or longer prayer times. We may be calm and peaceful or distracted and noisy; we are sad or glad, still or uneasy. We listen to the direction of the Lord perceived in the various movements of our bodies and minds. If we have rigid ideas about how our prayer times will go, then we can't allow any feelings of sadness or ennui, joy or celebration, that haven't been programmed by our own contrivances.

We need to admit that prayer is not for keeping God apprised of our activities, nor for our checking in on occasion, nor is it for comforting a God who is lonely without us. These notions of prayer make no sense to the contemplative who is never apart from God. The contemplatives approach God not for fireside chats but to stay in contact with their own identity. This purpose is not an exercise in navel-gazing but rather indicates that the contemplative wishes consistently to recall that all of life is lived in the context of God's life, and that daily commitment to Christian practice is essential. To be careless about the requisites of the message of Jesus is to threaten the truth of the spiritual journey with self-constructed religious illusions.

The contemplative cannot lead an unexamined life. Reflective prayer is steadfast no matter what the means; in fact, methods drop away as prayer becomes simple, free, and freeing. It is gradually becoming what we are, more than what we do. A contemplative knows with certainty that prayer is less something for God's sake than it is for our own. God will elude any and all of our narrow and confining ideas.

Sometimes we think we need prayer when what we need is recuperation. We lead busy, often burned-out lives and when we finally get to the roof and decide that this is our time for prayer, what we really need is sleep, a drink, or a bit of mindless TV in order just to let our bodies relax. Obviously, God does not mind our coming to prayer worn out, but there is no particular virtue in approaching prayer in an exhausted state. Prayer, like most of life, demands some common sense. If we lead our lives always panting to catch up with ourselves, then we don't need prayer; we need some help in discerning how we're using potential energies wastefully. A friend or a counselor could, perhaps, show us how to change some things.

The ancient Greeks knew that contemplation demanded the leisure mind. Josef Pieper suggests to us that the leisure mind is the one satisfied with itself; it has nothing to do with lots of free time. If there are radical insecurities which keep us dissatisfied with ourselves and which eat up our life's energies, we will be tired and depressed many times and will wonder why prayer doesn't change our circumstances. One doesn't need a degree in counseling to assess this situation. We must get a few affairs ordered. Prayer can flourish as long as we know how to sift pain and weariness into God. It is when we try to pretend to ourselves, God, and all others that all is well, that prayer becomes only another impossible and exhausting duty.

We probably all need a large dose of letting go of control in regard to prayer. We have somewhere along the line developed the notion that prayer is a skilled performance during which we must stick to the subject, get some ideas about it into our heads, and feel happy at the end because we have put in the time. Thus, while we're busy constructing our lives of holiness, the eternal God waits quietly for us to be finished with our personal program. Then Providence can open the possibilities of who we are to become when we get out of the way and are emptied of our pre-conceived notions about the whole enterprise. We can know prayer that is simple, free, and freeing as we gradually shift gears into letting God act and direct rather than continuing to glory in our own performances.

Of course, when we do not perform in prayer as we have presumed we ought, when we do not pray at all, or not enough, then we give ourselves permission to expend psychic energy in guilt. This is a wonderful, time-wasting pastime which keeps us excused from more important issues. This kind of useless guilt can occupy us for hours, days and years with an inconsequential, non-requiring repentance. It is so small of us. While we're fiddling along, God waits to summon us to authentic interiority.

Christian prayer ultimately becomes the prayer of Jesus rather than prayer to Jesus. As our experience of God in the entirety of life broadens and takes an ever more authentic Christian direction, we speak less to Jesus because our lives are becoming identifiable, in our own experiences, with that of Jesus. The name of Jesus may and does rise frequently to our lips, yet our primary experience is that of becoming of one mind and one form (as John Chrysostom says) with Jesus. The life of the Lord has begun to seep into every crack and corner of our reality. The contemplative thinks in, and acts out of, the whole complex that is faith. The prayer of perspective prepares one for this posture toward reality. The reflection demanded will require that we face ourselves, not allowing lies and manipulations to consume our days. Many voices in the Church are suggesting what this looks like in very practical ways. We deceive ourselves to our own peril as maturing women or men. Anthony Padavano wrote some years back that prayer is less a matter of saying the right words than it is of trying to live for the right reasons.

There are so many ordinary events in each day in which we have no particular sense of God's presence; if anything, most daily happenings seem godless. The toast burns, there is a quick and impatient argument, the phones ring, the typing gets finished and we call in the orders for the next day. We tote the barge and lift the bale and try to behave decently toward others. One day ends, another begins. Faith demands that we live with eyes that perceive the divine dimension in all this ordinary detail. A faith assessment usually does not occur in the moment of the ordinary, but in the sum of it.

The individual parts of our lives begin to fit together over many years. Indeed God has acted to save. Though much is humdrum, we know quietly and deeply that life is significant. In a mysterious way, we are being drawn into that accessibility of God manifest in the ordinary. God's accessibility is usually inaccessible because it is so ordinary we walk right past it.

We often wish it were different. We wish religious experience were a matter of lights and visions, of voices and clear directions. But faith is faith, not sight. "Blessed are those who have not seen and yet believe." However, there is a confirmation of meaning that gladdens us as we begin to interpret our times with faith. We recognize we are learning to pray the prayer of presence. We look back and see how we have changed. We have been brought to the place we are now. As we meet others, we are less out of touch with who and what they are. Yes, quietly and imperceptibly through the years, God has broadened each one of our narrow perspectives.

Traditionally we have called the prayer of presence the prayer of quiet. Somewhere, we've heard of this and our vague recollection is that the prayer of quiet was something Teresa of Avila or other saints were able to do. We picture them overcome in a swoon of silent adoration. Whatever it was all about, it is more than likely a million light years away from our struggling efforts to come before the Lord.

The meaning of the prayer of silence must be reinterpreted in order that, once again, we know this prayer to be not only the experience of a few saints, but something familiar to all those who faithfully try to follow the Lord. The rhetoric of the contemplative tradition can be translated appropriately into terms coherent with our present spiritual direction.

The prayer of quiet presumes a life which, however inarticulately, is definitely christianized. All decisions proceed from the convictions one has about what a redeemed yet sinful world is, about our call to involvement in it, and about the mandate given that in the end we must have learned to love. These thoughts need not be uppermost in one's consciousness but they are the foundation of the life of the contemplative and it is out of them that the Spirit and we shape our days. We may only infrequently advert to this foundation, yet we know that it is out of these definite convictions that life is lived. This kind of contemplative person is able to pray the prayer of quiet.

There are certain accurate statements we have read about the prayer of quiet: the contemplative experiences God as immanent both in presence and in absence. There is a stillness about the prayer of the contemplative; there are no words with which this person addresses God. There is a deeply silent, conceptless awareness of the unutterably, transcendent God. Such statements convey to us the highest of religious ecstasies. It is necessary to inquire into what they look and feel like in an ordinary day.

First, we have to refuse to let our imaginations take the old familiar pathways of interpretation and open our minds to the very real truth that the descriptions probably indicate that contemplatives have no words with which to explain what the whole of life is about. We can't say who God is to ourselves or to any others. When we read that the contemplative experiences God as radically present to life, we think: "Well, that must be nice. I can hardly get hold of God at all." The sentence does not imply that the contemplative goes around in a hot air balloon, filled with light and joy. The silence and the quiet which names the highest form of prayer must be understood in terms of the experience of conceptlessness. That's a big word which says we have no thoughts in our head. Contrary to a sort of human dullness or sluggishness, conceptlessness in this context refers to the fact that although faith assures that all of life is lived in the context of the reign of God, most of the time we have no great feelings of devotion about this during work or prayer. Moreover, we find ourselves on most occasions without even any cleverly or aptly formed ideas about God at all. We don't think of ourselves as contemplatives. Yet we live with some uncanny sense that life is lived in the ambiance of God.

Rarely, perhaps, we have some overwhelming sense of the power of God as a conflagration of life, but mostly what burns us up are the tasks of each day which consume our strengths. Then we feel ashamed. We ought to pray. The daily grind and God are felt as utterly separate. We dissociate life and prayer. We presume the prayer of quiet has no meaning for us; it is obviously only for people of great leisure.

This is the experience of conceptlessness for the contemplative, an experience of the emptiness of nowhere and nothing. These two words are aptly selected by the author of *The Cloud* in answering the questions of those who wish to learn to pray. They ask where they should be and what they should be thinking during prayer. The answer is that when one comes to prayer, one should be nothing and nowhere. Nothing and nowhere! Immediately we presume that in these words there is hidden some mysterious, wordless delight in which contemplatives bask. Perhaps so, but it is that delight experienced in the wisdom of not knowing and of knowing that not to know is at once everything and nothing of the mystery of God.

We must probe these words for what is ordinary about them. John Howard Griffin writes a description of the morning prayer of Thomas Merton. The monk said the psalms, of course, but he also said the psalms of making coffee, scratching of a skin rash, of coughing and sneezing, and of sweeping the cabin. To him all these psalms were the same; no one activity was more or less important than the other.

This portrait captures the presence nature of the prayer of silence. Thomas Merton said the psalms, yes, but he also swept the cabin, coughed and made coffee and all of this was his prayer. His days and nights were contemplative in their conceptless union with God and in the silent awareness of presence. His daily moments were silent and conceptless in the sense that he did not continually advert to any particularly godly thoughts, neither in making or drinking the coffee nor in reading the psalms. Contemplative prayer is so ordinary. Everything moves into a single focus. Sticklers for rational categories are bothered with this seeming lack of distinctions. But for the contemplative everything in life except sin becomes integrated and one in the Lord, yet inarticulate, unutterable, conceptless for much of the time.

Certainly there are specific times when the contemplative prays the prayer of perspective. Preachers often inveigh against those who say that "our work is our prayer." These homilists seem intent on tracking down any who do not put in time at prayer or meditation. The basic premise of the talk is a distortion of the reality of contemplation which is prayer within life. Contemplatives have no doubts that they must take time for reflection, that they must pray with others, that they need space and solitude so that their lives be not unexamined, foolish, wasted, scattered and disoriented. The contemplative, above all persons, knows the need for, and is never far from, a reflective life.

But the contemplative also knows that prayer is not

measured quantitatively. If we are serious, thinking human beings, then we know the need to reflect upon life in order to recognize the manifestations of God. We make mistakes; we may for some time think we can get by without serious reflection, without challenging reading, without prayers, or without solitary moments. But the quality of the prayer of presence is shallow or full in proportion to the deepening quality (not quantity) of the prayer of perspective.

The contemplative knows peak experiences and aridity, yet within both these states is a steadfast, if inarticulate, faith that God has acted once and for all in human history in Jesus. The gift of love cannot be withdrawn. Everything human has been forever sanctified. Whether our present mood is depression or elation, contemplation depends on faith and not on feeling good about oneself. In difficulty or in merriment, the contemplative confirms the presence of God in personal, ecclesial, and global history.

When we come to the small amount of time we have been able to set aside to gain some perspective, we find ourselves often exhausted and sometimes self-conscious as we begin our prayer. We are prepared to do menu-planning for the week or plot the airline schedule for the next business trip. We start a few prayers, leftovers from childhood. If we sit quietly, there seems to be nothing happening. We are afraid of the remoteness which surrounds life. Karl Rahner, in a beautiful Christmas meditation, urges us to enter into that remoteness knowing the Lord who is far and near at the same time. Merton speaks of entering the apex of one's mind and sitting there with the tranquil God who makes all things tranquil. We must train ourselves as we enter into prayer not to talk to ourselves or attempt to talk to God. We are not to carry on imaginary dialogues with absent friends or relatives. We must demand of ourselves that we be alone and confront the loneliness or the emptiness which the solitude bears.

Most all of our expectations about what should happen within us during a time of stillness are futile expectations. We think that perhaps some great joy, some sense of peace, some insightful thought about God and life will occur to us and we are discomfited when we are nowhere and nothing. We begin to blame ourselves for not paying attention, for day-dreaming, or for allowing distractions. These preoccupations may indeed characterize our ordinary lack of presence to people and situations each day and so they also shape our inability for presence to the Lord in prayer. But if we are persons who try to be present to life, then we will find ourselves present to our prayer in just the same degree. This statement, although true, does not thereby insure any great feelings of devotion.

The prayer of quiet is a time of identification of who we are and what we are about. We sit quietly. Life, joy, pain, and struggle are all before the Lord. Integrations and moments and years of disintegration are in the Lord. Life is a process through which we are led to the fullness of our humanity. Though it may often feel like it, life is not an absurdity catapulting from one day to the next. At center, the contemplative is rooted and grounded in God, yet faith in this truth does not change the routine of each day. The trials are still trying, the struggles still exhausting, the joys still surprising. All of the days are in God. The confidence is born in us that life with all its mysteries is not ultimately absurd. In the prayer of silence, without concepts, words or feelings, we confirm our lives. We shift gears into a faith acceptance of the days.

Often, in this prayer, we know disgust with ourselves or with others—a loneliness, a despair, or the presence of many unresolved conflicts. Sometimes when we can bring ourselves to it, or more accurately, when the Lord brings us to it, we pray for the endurance to stay with the prayer of quiet in a waiting attitude. We resist the temptation to run out for a sandwich or scrub the bathroom, and thus turn away from the silence. We choose to endure and embrace the silence and the conceptlessness.

A French Oratorian of the 17th century, Louis Thomassin, wrote a Dogmatic Theology one small part of which discusses the apex of the human mind, a topic pertaining to the silence and remoteness which surrounds the mystery of God. We have a highpoint of our humanity which we enter in our prayer, a place where in utter stillness we know God. This human antechamber to the Holy is an idea that has fascinated many spiritual writers both inside and outside Christianity. In digest, the ideas of Thomassin are these:

1.) The apex of the human mind is the primary and highest place of knowing God. It is this intellectual faculty which perceives God most immediately.

2.) God is one and simple beyond all negations or affirmations we can make. God is different from and beyond the apex of the human mind.

3.) We comprehend the ideas of the truth and the charity of God. But it is as we enter into and experience single-mindedness that we are able to touch most closely the simplicity which God is.

4.) Any symbols we may have for God, goodness, wisdom, or truth, are veils by which God is hidden. It is in the silent apex of the mind that we come to God beyond these symbols.

5.) This apex of our minds is a hidden sanctuary. Nothing profanes it and it is dedicated only to this hidden way of knowing.

6.) In the apex of my mind, God is known without words or thoughts. Herein the incomprehensibility of God is nearest to us.

7.) We may sing praises to God, but they will be empty, unless we have come to know the silence of the apex of the mind. This is the place where God is met without words.

We must make certain that these words of Thomassin (which he says represent the thought of Gregory of Nyssa, Augustine, Anselm, Dionysius, Maximus the Confessor, and others) do not take the prayer of quiet out of our ken. The emphasis is on silence, on a hidden way of knowing, and on God apprehended without words or thoughts. It is the nowhere and nothing experience again. We want to aggrandize what silently sitting in the apex of the mind connotes. We feel that only very recollected and holy people can enter this inner sanctuary. We presume all this because when we come to the prayer of quiet, it seems that we experience nothingness rather than devotion and so we return to active prayers: saying the rosary, saying the psalms, going to Mass. These engage us so that after completing them we feel like we have accomplished something.

But God is one. In the apex of our minds we know an integration of mind, body and spirit. It is an integration characterized by nowhere, nothingness and darkness in the sense of ordinariness. It is imperative that we understand experientially the ordinariness of the prayer of quiet and of the life of prayer. In the prayer of quiet, some fragments may fall into unity. The oneness which we then experience approximates as closely as humanity can the unity of God. But personal integrity is hard won. Faith tells us that God is bringing it about in us despite our usual feelings of fragmentation. The evaluation of the truth of our prayer has always been and continues to be the quality of our prayer of presence to each and every person and situation in the midst of our busy lives. Anything else named prayer is an illusion.

In the Chinese classic, Chuang Tzu, the author, records a fictitious conversation between Confucius and Yen Hui concerning fasting. Yen Hui presumes that Confucius means fasting from food. Confucius wants to clarify that he is speaking about the fasting of the heart. He says to Yen Hui that the goal of such fasting is inner unity. It will mean that one is emptied of the complex of motivations and banalities which fill foolish heads. In his conclusion to the dialogue, Chuang Tzu has Confucius say that when one succeeds with this fasting of the heart, one is utterly able to go among all persons with a sensitivity and a presence which allows them to be who they are, yet which challenges and calls them to the full potential of their giftedness.

With characteristic wisdom the Chinese author precisely captures the way to pray the prayer of presence.

Fasting of the heart allows one a freedom from foisting personal notions about everything upon the whole world. Because one is emptied, one is able to be filled with the truth of the present situation. We are able to find the most deft way and the exact moment to reach out to another in a way the person can or needs to be touched. We are sensitized to life. We no longer go after situations and people with the bludgeons of control, deceit, or craft. We meet another with honesty and openness. We can listen to each other's songs. The faculties of mind and senses are emptied of our own pretensions; unity and integrity can occur. So often what we call nothing and which worries us, is in fact part of the process of emptying. We begin to lose our preliminary antipathies about everything under the sun, and through the power of God, move toward a more single-hearted presence. The advice of Chuang Tzu does not bless a laissez faire attitude toward social involvement; it certainly does depict the wise person's classic ability in relationship.

The prayer of quiet, the prayer of presence, fasting of the heart, silent sitting, entering the apex of one's mind, all are metaphors for achieving the human potential of integration, of reconciliation, and of utter liberty. In the prayer of perspective we can integrate some of the complexities which fill our days. Some wordless ability to resolve ambiguity in the center of our being forms within us.

We prevent maturation in prayer because we are so reluctant to trust the direction our lives are taking. We move away from prayer because we are unwilling to give up our compulsive obsession to control and manipulate it. We can't let go trying to make ourselves good and seeing that those around us become religious as well according to the way we have determined it will all work together.

Our scriptures tell us that we possess a treasure which is Christ the Lord in an earthen vessel so that we will finally know that the power which brings us to maturation is God's power and not the natural human energy which we can muster up. The physical and mental dynamic we experience of shaping our lives, of reviving ourselves from the crush of affliction, of overcoming the despair of doubt, of rising from the abandonment of persecution, of refusing to let ourselves be destroyed, all these efforts on our part, St. Paul tells us, come from the power of God. They are the evidences of the treasure that lies at the center of the earthenware vessel: Jesus the Lord. Everything daily and so very ordinary is recapitulated in Jesus Christ.

It takes a long time in the spiritual journey to know the gradual transfer in our feeling-level from that of operating out of our own skills at fashioning the clay to the recognition that it is only the power of God which sustains us and which causes us to rise from the situations which could destroy us humanly. In the apex of our minds, we know the divine possibilities which lie within. Faith awakens. Jesus became a partaker of our humanity so that we might become partakers of his divinity. Making coffee, sneezing and coughing, talking to one I love, and the integration of all of these before the Lord through many years comprise the life of prayer.

CHAPTER SEVEN

The Experience of Today

THERESE OF LISEAUX helps us in our quest for understanding the contemplative life when she tells in her autobiography that she knew moments of contemplation far more often in her work than during her prayer. At her tasks in the monastery to which she gave all her attention and in which she was completely absorbed, she experienced a total concentration that approximated the unity of being that characterizes contemplation. Whether we are commuters in the networks of subways, or work in fields, office, or home, the demand of the daily schedule is part and parcel of the contemplative life.

Therese of Liseaux teaches us this, and her insight is corroborated by many others including persons so scattered in history as Augustine, Benedict, Jean Pierre de Caussade and the Zen Buddhists, to name just a few. What do all these have in common? The insights of these persons reflect what is inscribed on a particular bell: "I am what I do." They knew, without articulating it in just this way, that what we are and what we do must be focused. If we compartmentalize sacred and secular, work and prayer, relationship and solitariness, and if we have no inner mechanisms to join these passing moments, one with the other, we experience life as separated into portions which have no connection one with the other. Nor does one event offer any meaning to another.

The Zen Buddhist phrases this unity of being in terms of overcoming the relationship between subject and object. The archer becomes the arrow in order to hit the bull's eye. The flower arranger, in ordering flowers and rocks in an intricate and unified relationship, is one with the ordering of the cosmos. The celebrant of the ceremony of tea senses a convergence of the ambiguities of human existence in this ritual moment. The disparity of subject and object cease. The archer, the arranger of flowers, the celebrant of tea, and the contemplative know the integrity of the now and the precious aspect of today.

Augustine's acknowledgment that the essence of wisdom is simply to be resonates in the soul of the contemplative. Neither past nor future pertains to wisdom. To be is both eternal and present. The phenomenon we call contemplation is mysteriously connected with the eternal oneness, simplicity and presence, which God is. The contemplative has the wisdom of knowing that the present moment is the meeting place of the divine and human. "I am what I do."

When Benedict wrote his famous directive, "work and pray," he did not envision a dichotomy between the two. It is incongruous to imagine a monk of age and grace saying some prayers, then doing some work, then returning to the conventual chapel to recite some psalms, and then going back to work without any sense of the integration of all of this. The great spiritual father knew that duality was always becoming one in the maturing religious who was engaged in work and prayer simultaneously each moment of the day. "Do what you are doing," was the monastic adage that blessed one's total attention to the present. The path to this simultaneity is not a matter of doing one's tasks while reciting certain prayers or saying the Morning Offering before starting to work. Though both might be worthwhile practices, beyond them lies the wisdom that knows that daily choices will reflect the quality of prayer and that times of prayer will identify an authentic, Christian life.

Often, out of unconscious self-rejections, we position ourselves over against reality; we endure an alienation from ourselves and from the other. When these separations can be overcome, we find a new integrity which feels right with our humanness. We are ordered once again; the former chaos of multiple and ill-assorted pieces seems to be forming some whole. Now the moments of meeting, whether with a person, a task, a book, or the Lord become times of bonding in which otherness is gradually overcome. In his book, *Abandonment to Divine Providence,* Jean Pierre de Caussade named these moments as sacrament. The present is sacred because it is a happening which faith acknowledges as the locus of divine activity. All the faculties of our humanity converge in this sacrament of the present moment. We are ready and open to the meeting with the other. Presence is possible. By the transforming power of God and through many years, if we have allowed it, the integrity of being which is called contemplation is being wrought in us. Modern psychological tools can measure a person's time consciousness and computerize the results to show that in fact one either lives in the present (which is measured as a positive value), or one lingers somewhere in the past, or that one wistfully dreams oneself into an ethereal tomorrow.

We respect a person whose actions and whose intentions (which motivate the actions) are in correspondence. When the opposite is true, we are repelled by a deceit which is strangely apparent. In traditional ascetico-mystical literature, we read about purity of act or intention as an evidence of human holiness. God is described as Pure Act by the scholastics. Thomas Aquinas speaks of God as utterly simple; the effects of God resemble God imperfectly since they manifest in complexity what is in origin One and Simple. In the play, *A Man for All Seasons,* Robert Bolt relates that God looked for splendor among what was created but found there only complexity. Abraham Maslow names as self-actualized those of very great integrity who do what they are and whose potential functions maximally for this particular time of their lives. All these statements are a search after the same wisdom. Humanity approximates the nature of God in the journey away from fragmentation to integration. We try to reduce the complex webs of motivations woven around our actions. We give a gift because we hope we'll receive one in return. We reach out in love to others because we have deep needs for others to love us. Our ruses are numerous and oftentimes unconscious. But by God's redeeming power we achieve a few integrated plateaus. Sometimes we know why we do what we do, and we come nearer to closing the gaps between what we are and what we do. In proportion to the truth of our integration process, we touch the simplicity of God. It is for ultimate Unity that we are created.

The Experience of Today

Is this course set before us as some vast cosmological joke? Why, if God wanted us *one,* were we created with bodily and mental faculties which scatter our energies in all directions? What is the divine madness that will watch the complex try to become simple against odds that thwart our efforts?

We come from God and go back to God. The yearning the contemplative has for union arises from that mysterious obediential potency which the human has for the divine. Apparently we possess a natural instinct for returning to our own centeredness which is the antechamber of the divine: "Our hearts are restless until they rest in Thee." Augustine's famous sentence underscores our discontent with complexity. Fragmentation increases as we move farther from the meeting place of divine and human. Jesus experienced this unity uniquely and supremely; we come to it by divine adoption because we are loved.

Our complexities are comprised of the network of psychological strengths and weaknesses, physical strengths and weaknesses, motivations, rationalizations, confusions, and of course, the growing awareness of the mortality which announces our human diminishment. The fact of our mortality frightens us when we think about it, yet it helps us be realistic about the fact that neither in the complexities of our bodies nor of our world do we have anything that will last.

Although the knowledge and experience of fragmentation threatens to overwhelm, the contemplative knows that the Lord is One. Dionysius suggested centuries ago that the Divine Unity contained all things, combining even opposites into the form of oneness. In faith, we believe that even the polarities we know within ourselves will be eventually reconciled. This reconciliation is our constant search and our steadfast hope. The path to integrity is arduous precisely because it does not circumvent our humanity. We are made as we are, other than the Creator, yet a creation always yearning toward its origin. It is at once our glory and our pain to render into one, by God's love, the fragments of our humanity and so to become that which God is.

Some will charge that this is some kind of Neo-Platonic doubletalk. To enunciate the nature of contemplation one is always forced to do battle with words that separate as well as to withdraw from words that imply numerical identity. Yet, through all the centuries, many have desired to tell of the contemplative reality, no matter the dilemma of a proper language. The challenge to explicate a life of such extraordinary religious simplicity occurs again every time unusual pieties and devotions start to eclipse what is ordinary and daily.

We experience a growing integrity in proportion to the spontaneity of our acts and decision. Ignatius referred to a highly integral state of mind in his pertinent examples of how and when people make proper choices. He described the situation of greatest integrity of act as that in which one moves to a choice without hesitation after the obvious path has been discerned. This lack of hesitation characterizes the spontaneity of movement which is the hallmark of the contemplative. We do not labor at inserting meaning into our actions, nor do we operate in a stilted manner, nor are we ill at ease and uncomfortable in social situations. The contemplative is lost in life, lost in God within life, lost in the prayer of presence and lost in the humdrum and the shuffle of today. St. Paul speaks of our being a praise of God's glory. Movements, thoughts, work, routine, process, unfolding, prayer, tossing the salad, and we ourselves, in all these moments, are a praise of God's glory. The experience of being lost in life is the experience of conceptlessness. Therese said the absorption happened mostly while she was working; we recognize in it very ordinary circumstances. We have known times when we were completely involved in what we were doing. We had no concepts in our minds. We were not watching ourselves doing the thing. We were not thinking about ourselves or wondering whether anyone else was watching us or not. We were simply attentive and present to the moment. We cut the grass, or fished, or played the banjo, or talked to the lady next door. All of who we are was together in the moment. We have had to learn to name this integrity an experience of contemplation.

This of the quality of hospitality. We can recall being received by someone who was obviously not happy to see us. No real concern or welcome was given but merely a minimal observance of stereotypical social rituals. We've had the opposite experience of being greeted graciously by those who offered us their presence. The contemplative meets another without self-consciousness. If, because of our exhaustion or lack of time, the guest may be turned away, the honesty of the dialogue is able to be comprehended by the other. Thus, in any ritual, whether of church or society, the contemplative is the one who, with exquisite balance, blends internal with external. It is a fusion perceivable even to the most casual observer.

We might well be worrying: "We are not together in our todays. Most of the time we are not what we do, nor do we do what we are." The true contemplative knows, however, that human integration occurs only very gradually through many years and many experiences. We have learned to wait, not futilely for a Godot who never comes, but in simplicity and hope for the light that transforms and transfigures. There may be years of indecision and questioning that must be endured. There may be a frightening sense of doubt and embarrassment about the direction life seems to be taking. The contemplative waits for inner knowledge, yet in the waiting reaches out to others with genuine receptivity—a characteristic which in itself assures the confirmation of one's existence.

The Rule of Taize marks as events of transfiguration those times in which one begins to see light in the midst of darkness. As we gain the ability to accept the shadows in ourselves and others, we admit the light of Jesus Christ which transfigures the shadows about which we alone are able to do nothing. The contemplative experiences the transforming occurrence of transfiguration and the presence of the One who transfigures. The alteration of personality is not achieved by human powers asserting further energies but is brought about by a divine dynamism which grants within us the transfiguring possibility to continue.

The only leisure needed for contemplation is a fundamental attitude of being at home in our world, reasonably content with who we are and what we do, and possessing some basic understanding that we and the entire community of humankind are in the process of becoming whole by God's plan. We are weak, limited, and sinful, but we believe that our time unfolds, by the power of grace, into potentially growthful directions and that we have something to do with the creation of our future.

A leisure mind is directly related to an openness and eagerness to life's evolving summons to change. If our days are constituted by the banal and the static, we will need some cleansing storms to sweep away our apathies. When we have eliminated any occasions to do things differently, we have usually resisted precisely those opportunities that might have stretched our thought and captivated our imaginations into fresh challenges. Have we recently changed our hair style or chosen a different tie? Have we driven to work a different way or tried a new recipe? Obviously these are minimal deviations from established patterns but they evince the fact that one meets the day with some modicum of vitality and novelty. We must pray against the blind spots of cast-iron, immovable, and rigid antipathies.

We stereotype role models to the degree that we cannot even conceive a notion that a Martin could and should know how to crochet a pot holder or a Maureen could change a tire. When our world is too small, our potentialities atrophy because we have employed perhaps only ten percent of their maximum. We reject ourselves as creative people to the degree that we reject the knowledge that our gifts are unique and important. The liberation of both women and men from the narrow roles which our acculturation has caused, is a part of a dream for a future in which Church and society can alter their self-understandings. Perhaps the contemplative will be accused of being a dreamer, but it is stimulating and inventive to dream great dreams and to do all one can do to make them come true.

At the end of a day, the contemplative remembers the happy moments and the errors in a closing moment of reflection and examination. We continue to choose life. This act of recollecting is the last act of the day. It lasts perhaps only a few seconds; we do not dredge up painful memories but we cast the day into the healing power of God. Perhaps by Christ's redeeming forgiveness, the gap between what we are and what we do has been in some ways overcome. We can praise the greatness of God who transfigures our dust and nothing into fields and fruits, an image used by Thomas Merton in his "Whitsun Canticle" to speak of the transforming activity of God's moving Spirit.

An issue congruent with the contemplative's experience of today is the movement toward a simpler lifestyle. Voices from the Third and Fourth Worlds as well as national and religious leaders have called us to change. In addition to overcoming internal fragmentation, we long to unravel the external complexity of our lives which entangles us in ever diminishing freedom.

The search for a simpler lifestyle is in itself not simple, but our yearning for the One compels our questioning the extravagances of our present lifestyle. When we have strayed quite far from the meaning which a Christian imputes to life, we forget our identity, our purposes, and our interconnection in the Lord with our global neighbors. The many calls to a simpler lifestyle help us to re-examine our vocation to discipleship. We have been asked to work toward a redistribution of the world's resources and for the establishment of a new economic order. Can we legitimately refuse to critique our present economic system as if all were right with our world? The call to discipleship may include standing counter even to the values which have formed our present identity.

We know only too well that a minority of the world's population, most of whom espouse the Christian faith, presently consume an overabundance of the world's resources. Our faith and our overconsumption are glaring inconsistencies between what we say and what we do. This dichotomy can only result in a gathering sense of absurdity regarding the nature and implications of religious faith.

We prosper on selling complexity. If our desire to consume goods lessens, the entire economic system is threatened. We can never stop building better mousetraps that someone will want to buy, even while we buyers of mousetraps can hardly find ways to divest ourselves of all the mousetraps with which our homes are cluttered. Advertising pits itself against our personal insecurities, sustaining in us a hope that some product will fill up what is lacking in us. We presume that what we buy can cushion our lives against the blows of our own inadequacies and dissipate our inabilities to relate to others. The call of the church to examine justice issues and to change social ills indeed demands that we think about adopting a simpler lifestyle.

The contemplative seeks an external simplicity because we place bonds on our humanity by what we possess. The more we have, the less free we become to move, to be disciples, to discover the needs of our world and to reach out to them. This claim presumes, of course, that our desire to follow in Jesus' path is a true one chosen by us as believing adult Christians. When we have many possessions, we can insulate ourselves against intrusions. We do not witness war, violence, or hunger except on television, and sometimes we choose not to watch films like "Roots" or "Holocaust" or see movies about Vietnam because we are unable to look at the radical insecurities which others experience as facts of life. We need to allow ourselves the feelings of horror and anger which can compel us to hunger and thirst after justice as the Gospel dictates.

Our possessions, our neighborhoods, and our security guards deprive us of the freedom to preach and to heal except in very limited spheres. Certain subtle agents usually manage to keep us fairly well-sheltered within familiar circles, the first of which is, of course, our own rationalizations for excusing ourselves from thinking about social issues at all. Secondly, the institutions of which we are a part—family, neighborhood, church, particular towns or cities—have customs and lifestyles into which we have been inculturated. These institutions facilitate our social grouping, give us identity, and enable us to accomplish corporate purposes. We must not, however, be so locked into our structures that we are unaware of people and customs outside our milieu. We have to live within definite systems but we must do this with a constant awareness of the encroachments which our institutions make upon our yearnings for a change of lifestyle. "We've always done it this way." "This person is not one of us," or "Surely you're not going into that neighborhood!" These are the cliches of our patterned exclusions.

We experience the Church as an institution through which the followers of Jesus have been able to accomplish many good works for the alleviation of human miseries. The institution is responsible for leadership and social services but most of all for the gathering of the faith community. We cannot cast off the requirements of socialization and koinonia in an effort at individuality cut off from ecclesial relationships. It is naive to attack the Church as institution with the idea that it could or should be deinstitutionalized. However, excessive and unexamined institutionalization is what permits presumption, sloth, and triumphalism to halt the efforts of the Church in renewal. Though we are always part of the institution, we must de-institutionalize our minds enough so that, as a people, we can retain a measure of freedom in following Jesus, whose imperative for the kingdom of God is a present mandate incumbent upon each of us. The Christian life is a free choice of involvement in the mystery of God and God's relationship to humankind; the Christian life is certainly not a series of requirements placed upon us by those entrusted with the Petrine ministry. We have to evaluate repeatedly the dedication and commitment to the commission which Jesus gave us. Jesus cannot be put on the shelf as an historical object to be venerated and studied. Jesus must be reckoned with today. The institutions into which our lives are cast can, by their programmed possibilities (programmed if we permit it) militate against our searching after and choosing a simpler lifestyle.

The contemplative wonders whether we are mad even to ask these questions or to attempt experimenting with solutions, yet we sense that our complexities are destroying us. Happily, there seems to be some wind of the Spirit summoning us to deal with our world, not by flailing out foolishly and rashly, but by making the slow steady choices that might turn a civilization around. What agents of change are availabe to us?

Instead of scouring the house, closet, or office for something to donate to charity, we might commence our project by stressing the positive. We choose a path to a simpler lifestyle by training ourselves to value our own and other's gifts. List those things that are our riches of mind, body, and spirit. Take the time to name what is good, beautiful and gifted about out ourselves and about all those who are a part of our lives. Time? We're so busy we can hardly take the time to say hello.

The eyes that see find focus as we lure ourselves away from our own noise, from shopping malls, advertising gimmicks, and too much television. The time saved gives us the possibility to look with quiet appreciation at who and what we are. Each of us ought to be able to identify at least one person who has called recently not for business but just to be a friend. We don't have time. We can't allow anyone to care enough for us to become friend. We can't take the time to share life in order to trust, marvel, and rejoice at what is within ourselves and within another. Yet by concentrating on what is within, we can advance to a simpler way of walking in another's moccasins without the contrivances and social amenities that frequently characterize social relation-ships within institutions. We are able to be in touch with another's inner life and wisdom to the degree that we are in touch with our own.

By striving toward keener levels of appreciation and a heightened awareness of our world and its people, the contemplative learns to find beauty in broken concrete, in mounds of white or soot-blackened snow, in the quiet of a rural area, or the noise of a city; we find beauty in the power of rain when it floods viaducts and streets or in the gentle rain that waters gardens, plants, farms, and hot, dry people.

The contemplatives of the world can more easily than most give ourselves some moments of silence and reflection in which we are not finnagling our lives or someone else's into neatly controlled boxes. We can slough off, at least most of the time, the intrusions of banality in order to choose simpler pleasures, inner joys, and the small things about other people in which to revel. We will have to spotlight what invades our inner silences, pray to set these distractions aside, and allow ourselves the space to welcome ourselves and others.

The solitude gained frees the contemplative to focus psychic attention. We can fritter away a great deal of energy with inconsequential worries and miss the advent of so much of God's manifold creation in people and situations. Movement to a simpler lifestyle can allow us the leisure to single out issues which call for our collaboration. We can make small choices that will lead us away from the overabundance that chokes our life and freedom. We are less emotionally and mentally scattered when we take time to focus on our gifts. What is truly significant can take precedence on our list of priorities. Concern for our environment and the promise of a future to our posterity might arise out of our growing integration. We listen to the calls for disarmament and world peace; perhaps we can enter the arena of social involvement in order to bring some political action against unjust situations.

There are other agents which help us change long-established patterns. One of these is the permission of some discomfort into our ordinary circumstances. Without telling the whole world about it, we might content ourselves with something that is less than perfect or fashionable; we might do a piece of work with our hands instead of using an electric appliance. We might try to be content with less rather than more and to purchase what we need rather than what we want. None of these change agents will turn national security states into peace-seeking nations, but the contemplative knows a personal need to keep a razor-sharp awareness about the future of our planet and these small gestures at least prevent an infantile oblivion.

Mostly we find ourselves trapped by time schedules. We can't drive an old model car because we don't have time to fix a blowout on the way to the airport to catch the plane that's flying us to our next appointment. We haven't time to allot to the breakdown of machines or conveyances, let alone persons. We are the children of the computer age; the manual typewriter is no more. Without being antediluvian about it, we need to determine some alternatives.

The contemplative well knows the experience of walking around the issue rather than striking right at the heart of it. One solution is to locate some friends who might join us on the pilgrimage in order to strengthen mutual resolution. Our decisions might take on the character of prophecy in the faith community, because we might be able to interpret our times to others from the vantage point of our growing perceptions. Perhaps just making certain changes about the ways we do things will enable us to think more clearly, to see the directions society is taking, and to try to make a difference. Think of the changes in our routines if we didn't show up at the shopping mall for a couple of months or turned off the football games. Think of the time we might use more profitably if we started some of these personal boycotts. Shopping or TV are certainly not everyone's addictions but substitute any personal compulsions. Then eliminate some percentage of these and examine the possibilities for creative development in the ensuing leisure. Imagine the opportunities to look at what is beautiful around us, within us, and within our families and friends. Sadly, too many of us use the malls or television to hide from contact which we find tedious. This evidence of breakdown of relationship has its own problematic and its own cry for solution.

With the chosen group of friends, we might agree to meet and talk about all this once a month. We want to seek together for a simpler lifestyle and to move closer by the transforming power of God's grace to that simplicity which God is. We must stay with honest questions and possible solutions and report on any successes, struggles or failures in our attempts. The whole enterprise has to be cast into the hands of the Lord as we agree to go the distance with one another to dream the dreams of alternate futures.

Patience is essential as we seek realistic ways to live more simply. Just thinking through all the aspects of the questions is a tangle in itself. Gerard Manley Hopkins in his poem "Peace," knew the prior position of patience because he connects the desires for peace with this forerunner and necessary companion. He defines patience in terms of steadfast activity even in the face of alarms and fears of wars. But patience seems so infinitely slow. Why don't we change? Why don't our institutions change? How can we be the first to serve what is socially unacceptable, wear the clothes that aren't right, speak out in instances where people might judge us weird, or seek some direction in faith and by prayer? The contemplative makes deliberate choices away from the societal programming so aptly portrayed in current art forms. If we do not seize the freedom we have to think a different thought or to change long-established patterns, the probability of using our freedom will gradually ebb until we reach an age where we suffer the loss of the social structures which supported our deceits and we are cast on our own meager and insufficient inner resources.

If the thought of a simpler lifestyle causes only sour feelings and if our friends are only carping, complaining social critics, perhaps valuable energies are being wasted in useless conversation. In proportion to becoming simpler in person and lifestyle, we ought to perceive at the same time, that we are becoming more joyful. Joy connotes the best of childhood with its feasts and merry occasions. When we are not dragging all the baggage we've taken upon our hearts and minds, we can be free to be funny. We can find ourselves laughing more, not from the cynicism that was *de rigueur* in previous social situations, but from the deep wellspring of joy which is born of experience. We have felt personally the power of Rose Kennedy's words: "I will not be vanquished."

It seems that our choice for a simpler lifestyle is being made for us. The alternative is the destruction of ourselves and of our civilization. We can specify our own agents of change, but a basic decision to follow Jesus must be made in the most radical way we can conceive. St. Benedict described a kind of monk who floated on the surface of life without choice or decision. This monk was a drifter and a vagabond, one who never really entered into any relationship, who never really loved or was committed to anything except himself. He was one who drifted from one shallow purpose to another, a movement externally symbolized in his journey from one monastery to another. We can deny the facts. We can close the door on challenge and call. We can be content to play once again the five easy pieces we learned when starting piano lessons. But withdrawal is not the solution to complexity. The quest for a simpler lifestyle is resolved only in the graced ability of the contemplative woman or man who takes the struggle, the joy, the ambiguity, and the doubt in each day and brings them to integration in the center of one's own mind and heart by the power of God.

There is in Christian tradition a perennial admonition to flee the world. The present move toward increased socialization and interdependence seems in direct contrast. With the accent on integration and social responsibility, contemplatives have assumed a very different stance toward what we have previously called "the world." The laity used to be "in the world," while priests and nuns were not. The arena for the lay apostolate was the world, while the task for the religious was that of holiness. Things have changed, thank God! Now everybody is "in the world" and everybody seems to be called upon to do something about it.

John's gospel has Jesus saying some serious things about this universe in which we find ourselves.

> I have made your name known to those you gave me out of the world; for these I pray, not for the world. I gave them your word and the world has hated them for it.

> They do not belong to the world anymore than I belong to the world. As you have sent me into the world so I have sent them into the world that all may be one as you, Father, are in me and I in you. I pray that they may be one in us; that the world may believe that you sent me. Just Father, the world has not known you but I have known you and these men have known that you sent me.

The sentences seem to propose that his followers hide from the world lest their involvement in it would lead them away from the Lord. What did he mean?

Through the centuries many Christians have interpreted Jesus' words and acted out of the judgments they made. In the 11th century, Anselm spoke of the flight from the world in terms of abandoning the confusion of wars, hatred among families, or aimless wanderings as the kinds of violence and dissolution which the followers of Jesus must reject. Thomas Aquinas offered his tripartite explanation of the world: it is created by God and therefore it is good; it is completed, finished and perfected in Jesus; the world of peoples must become what Jesus is. Yet the world can be perverted and distorted; it is we ourselves who can destroy creation. Lately we have been feeling that perhaps our world is a gigantic, ungovernable mass plummeting to its destruction. As one disaster after another occurs, we become more perplexed as we try to sort out the pieces and to order the chaos even in our minds.

The contemplative asks whether the world is a reality over against us or something within us. Is the world to be abandoned or embraced? Is it a "thing" at all? We have endured the anguish of the violation of our world.

We've lived through unjust wars. We've watched a drug culture that has destroyed minds and bodies flourish. We've seen the effect of global injustice. Conversely, we've known love and friendship within and outside the immediate community of the family or church. We've witnessed movements for social change and rejoiced in persons whose lives speak of courage and commitment to everything that is great and good.

The *Jerome Biblical Commentary* contrasts the connotation of "world" in the classical tradition which John's Gospel reflects with that meaning found in the documents of the ancient Near East. The former conceived the world as an impersonal, objective unity with regular and predictable behavior governed by laws. The latter did not even have a word that could be so translated; the Semite simply knew the conflicting diversity of natural forces in which irregularity prevailed more than order. The unpredictability outside oneself corresponded with the unpredictability within. To order or arrange the disordered, one always had to compromise with ever-impending chaos.

The rhetoric of the subjective and the anarchic captures well the sense the contemplative has of the world. That one can order one's universe is always such a tenuous possibility, yet the Christian contemplative does not view the world as a malevolent, objective force. The incarnation forever embraced the world with its personal and social ills. Redemption is extended to each person as well as to the relationships which constitute society; there is, by reason of our faith in the incarnation, the salvific possibility for justice, freedom and peace. Salvation happens because there are those who extend God's life and truth into all the areas of death and darkness. The darkness that threatens both the individual and society is dispelled as we agree not only to endure our times but to embrace them.

The contemplative accepts the world knowing that its darkness exists within us, and that its redemption is connected with daily, faithful choices. The contemplative does not forsake the world which God assumed. With Anselm, we renounce war and hatred but recognize that these are within us as are the powers of goodness and grace. When our world, in its daily sinfulness, is abandoned in some misguided choice for God alone, a heresy against the meaning of the incarnation has again been inflicted on history.

Thomas Merton knew the contemplative did not make a choice between following Jesus or following something out there named the world. The contemplative chooses both and renounces only those aspects of ourselves which are alienated, rigid, closed, unconcerned and shallow. True solitude is found in self-presence. To flee or to leave the world in any authentic interpretation means to flee the alienation that we have chosen by our sin.

Contemplatives do not imagine looking out of the window at the world. We perennially question the worldview of commencement speakers who urge graduates out into the real world. The real world is always were the contemplative is. The world is myself and my life as it evolves. It is a mystery which continues to be created, to unfold, and to expand. We do not hypostasize or personify the world. Our lives and our world interpenetrate and, through a creative maturity, we shape and form in the same action the meaning of our lives and of our world. Through this creativity, we overcome estrangement from ourselves, from others, and from God.

The worldview of the contemplative is never pinched and cramped like a forlorn Alice in some tiny house. Each day bears the possibility of enlargement and extension of vision beyond preconceptions. One's worldview, suggests Karl Rahner, is the sum of all the pieces of personal history, experiences, philosophies, sinfulness and greatness, all embraced by the grace of God. The contemplative has learned to live graciously within the pluralism which comprises the self.

The contemplative moves through the world with a sense of wonder. Ours is the gentle ability to be aware of the extraordinary goodness of people, to be amazed at the way they survive personal anguish, and to be continually surprised by beauty. We are in touch with the child-spring within. We celebrate life and reject being witlessly swept along.

Because we bear the burden of responsibility for our world, we seek means to increase that sense of responsibility until we are finely honed instruments for justice. In the novels about the Yaqui Indian, Don Juan, the main character, refers to our responsibility for being here in this marvelous time, this marvelous world, this marvelous desert in which each act must count.

Our world will be as big as our psyche wants it to be. When we counter our pretenses, we can live with an exhilarating realism. In self-presence there is an inner stillness in which we create our world. Even in its worst turmoil, the world is a redeemed creation. The desire to be away from the storms and the swing of the sea articulated by Hopkins can't be read as a choice for a "heaven's haven" apart from our present history with its social responsibilities and its calls for justice. The contemplative reads the poem as a summons to enter into the self, to find there that one is rooted and grounded in God, and to know that the world evolves from this personal center.

The contemplative waits for God in each day with urgent patience. Since we have always understood the necessity of justice as constitutive of the preaching of the Gospel, we know the very real possibility of being the lamb of sacrifice whose life will be taken for justice's sake.

Perhaps it is not enough to write a letter to a congressperson, or boycott or demonstrate against excessive armament. Jesus spoke of giving one's life. Whatever this may entail—leaving loved ones, opinions, home, or lands for Jesus and for the sake of the Gospel—it is the contemplative who hears the summons and who responds as did most prophets, "Why me?" The contemplative is driven to justice by the power of the Lord whose threshing sledge eventually winnows all the grains of today. Here is the servant who is the ready instrument for justice. Sometimes this means something so ordinary as stating one's opinion at a parish meeting when it may be unpopular to do so. Other times, it may mean a great deal more. Whatever the form of prophecy, this person is being drawn by the Lord into deeper levels of commitment by the Christian way of life. The experience of today breaks out of patterns, lifestyles, neighborhoods, and any self-constructs that incarcerate the Spirit. Today is both frightening and marvelous. It holds the possibilities for death or life. We must choose life today, therefore, so that we and our descendants may live tomorrow.

CHAPTER EIGHT

The Experience of Church

THE church understood both as a people and as an institution is at once a joy and a sorrow for the contemplative. It is a bearer of faith and a test of faith. Its leaders and its people are both holy and sinful, self-sacrificing and self-serving. It is a social grouping of which we are at times blissfully proud and at other times painfully embarrassed. Our spiritual heritage is rich and filled with many ordinary and extraordinary people. Some were saints who built up the Body of Christ while others were evil-doers who deliberately brought harm to the community. The contradictions evident in the rhetoric express well the ambivalent experience the contemplative has of church. Here is a person unable to applaud the church unquestioningly yet unable to critique it to the point of disassociation.

How does one explain the anomaly of a people and its leaders which fascinates and disenchants simultaneously? Jesus gathered his followers, shared his life with them, and promised his presence to the evolving community to the end of time. This people grew and changed in a socially predictable manner. It is a completely human group of folks yet a church whom the Spirit of God empowers and directs. Since this direction is never other than in human terms, we perennially witness the foibles that are a part of the human situation of sinfulness and woundedness.

The catholic contemplative is a member of this 2,000-year-old church which is a people utterly free to follow the Lord and at the same time a people who have themselves created the sociological structures which sometimes impede that freedom. When criticized, it is usually the institutional structure that receives the verbal blows. Most of us, including our leadership, are not yet at home with referring to the people as church. We exclude ourselves linguistically, and therefore in reality, almost every time we speak the word. I am choosing deliberately to indicate people when I write church and to limit myself in discussing church to the religious experience a contemplative has of the mystery of the faith community. To examine this experience necessitates discovering the symbols by which a contemplative expresses the reality of church. If we easily grasp the symbols by which someone explains a reality, it means that we comprehend the reality in the same way, and that the symbols are valid. The more widely verified are the symbols, the more common is the understanding of the reality. We need to identify our current symbols for church or reclaim some ancient ones which will clarify who we are as a church people and what are the dimensions of our present mission. People express symbolically what they think and feel about themselves; thus our symbols for ourselves help establish our identity.

A valid symbol participates in the reality to which it points, since in itself, it communicates the reality. If we give a ring to a loved one, the meaning of the ring is clearly understood by both. The gesture lacks mutual significance if we hand a ring to a passer-by. It may be a paper one from a cigar, a metal one from the top of a can, or a diamond, but to the loved one, the ring holds within itself the unity of the love. It is a proper symbol; it identifies the nature of the relationship. If the love between us dies, and if we discover the ring many years later in a dresser drawer, we know that the symbol no longer retains the meaning that it once had. Though it may awaken some memories, the symbol has died because the reality it signified no longer exists.

A symbol that signifies a faith community must convey immediately the identity of that community to itself. In the collective unconscious of the members, the symbol captures the reality of the faith and needs no lengthy explanation. If someone were to suggest in a lecture that the reality of church is signified by a blue banana, even the most polite would have to answer with a resounding, no! A blue banana communicates no meaning to us. If a preacher announces that the meaning of church is adequately summarized by a fraternity or sorority house, the faithful would have to deny the symbolic value of this image borrowed from a college campus. It does not in any way convey the mission and message which Jesus gave his followers.

The early community had many ways to explain itself; Jesus had named them seed, flock, light, salt, rock, city on a mountain—all powerful images of a faith people. These scriptural symbols suggested a church summoned by the word of Jesus and confirmed in the mission of preaching and healing.

Very early in our tradition we find traces of military symbols. The writer of the epistle to the Ephesians speaks of putting on the breastplate of righteousness, the shield of faith, the helmet of salvation and the

sword of the Spirit. John Chrysostom refers to the cate-
chumens as soldiers of Christ. The Crusades, however
one may judge these unfortunate historical forays after
infidels, urged the followers of Jesus into battle for the
Lord with God on our side. Perhaps it was Ignatius'
personal experience as a soldier that gave his society a
military bearing, and the obedience of Jesuits to this
day retains a military aspect. In many of our personal
histories, the sacrament of Confirmation carried with it
the notion of becoming a soldier of Christ. So long did
this symbol prevail in Catholic history that many of us
can recall, during our high school years, singing the
lyrics: "An army of youth flying the standards of truth.
We're fighting for Christ the Lord!" For U.S. Catholics,
however, the recent experiences of war have all but ne-
gated the appropriateness of the military symbol.
Though "soldier" connotes daring, commitment and
bravery, the media has awakened us to many of its more
unworthy aspects. The military has become a symbol
which conveys an ambivalent message, and one the followers of Jesus do not wish to employ.

Symbols arise, explain reality to us for a time, and die
when the reality changes. It is pointless at best to cling
to symbols that have lost their meaning or to continue
to use a symbol that no longer truly expresses the reality
it is intended to signify.

For the 400 years between the Council of Trent and
the Second Council of the Vatican, many Catholics felt
themselves within an enclave, a fortress, or a castle
from which the rest of the world was excluded, except
through conversion. Within our own environs, we knew
clearly who we were and what we stood for. No matter
that we were not in touch with those outside the walls;

we had the truth and grace. All others were to come to the enclave in order to be saved. When John XXIII opened doors and windows, we knew, with some amount of pain and with a desire to close ourselves off again, that we had to answer many questions about our identity even to ourselves. The symbol of the sturdy and impregnable fortress had died. The unalterable reality of church was not what we had presumed. With great seriousness, outsiders were claiming to be followers of Jesus. They gave witness to their words by lives of extraordinary faith. Non-Christians also bore testimony to the importance and holiness of their creeds. Who were we Catholics? Those closest to the heart of God? Persons special and unique in salvation history?

Centuries before, our forebears had written about the dynamic nature of our baptisms. Why had we locked ourselves once again in upper rooms? The decade of the sixties propelled us into a world for which our current catechism proved inadequate. We are still recovering from the shock of this traumatic rebirth. Some of us want to go back; others intimate that we haven't even begun to make the changes necessary in church structures.

The time has come when it is imperative for us to establish our identity. We cannot exist without naming for ourselves, if not for others, who we are, what we stand for, and what our lives are all about. Our present experience of church is one of being between symbols. We have been forced to forego the symbols of the fortress, the enclave, or the castle, yet currently apt symbols are still in the process of evolving. We happen to be alive in a very difficult period of church history. Strong reactionary currents urge us to return to the good old days. Perhaps we really ought to re-establish the enclave and strengthen its walls, albeit benevolently and pastorally; tell outsiders that though we are kindly disposed toward them and anxious for their good, we are not part of them nor they a part of us. In the enclave we knew who we were, a western church with solid European roots.

Vatican II named us pilgrim. We U.S. citizens could be immediately happy with the designation. Pilgrims have had a big part to play in our history. The symbol spoke to us of turkey and pumpkin pie. It told of giving thanks and of happy feelings of warmth and family. We have learned, however, that we are far better tourists than pilgrims. A pilgrim marches along uncharted ways. This fundamental insecurity is perhaps proving more than we were equipped to bear emotionally and spiritually.

As pilgrims on dark and confusing paths, we often feel we've lost our way and our old identity. Anne McCaffrey's mythical dragons possess the secret of going between eons and geographical environs. We Catholic non-dragons are not too comfortable with the between times of history. If we can't assert who we are in the midst of the vagaries of pilgrimage, then let's return to captivity. We had it better in the old days. We knew our place and we stayed in it.

The symbol of pilgrim resonates in the heart of the contemplative. This person is accustomed to being open to life and to finding God within life. The contemplative knows that a pilgrim has an internal attitude of strength and consolidation no matter that history is filled with inexplicable occurrences. We have wandered through many personal pilgrimages to the center of our own existence. All external journeying thereafter is moderated by the wisdom of the previously experienced internal movement. The contemplative knows that the ultimate destiny is God. We know moments of loss of direction and the terrors of the way. There are obvious feelings of being continually uprooted and endless periods of questioning the reason for journeying at all; nonetheless, there is a fundamental sense of trust and dependence in the promise of the Lord who summons always to the mystery that is unknow and inexhaustible.

Thomas Merton wrote of the Irish pilgrims who set out, not to visit sacred shrines but, in exile from all they held dear, to search for God. They entrusted themselves to Providence. Though their journey took them into the irrationalities of winds and seas inside and outside themselves, it was a journey ultimately destined to a divinely appointed meeting place. The pilgrim is not a vagabond or an aimless and rootless wanderer.

In the 60's we began to feel that we were a pilgrim people, and we've had to learn many hard lessons about the symbol. It does not connote a timid and tattered group huddling together in a transit shelter, although sometimes we have given this impression of ourselves. We have had to learn that a pilgrim must walk with other pilgrims. This particular requirement obligates each of us to offer an explanation of the journey and some directions by which we will agree to chart our course. No one has been allowed to sit silently in the pews. We are to speak of what we see and through this corporate reflection and decision-making, discern what the Spirit is saying to the church. We gather together for prayer and to talk over the meaning of pilgrimage. We determine the direction of a parish or diocese and we make both worthy and erroneous judgments. We walk in the wrong direction for a while. We take false turns and have to turn back even when we have been marching on a particular path for a few years. Individually and corporately we meet the absurd in human existence. Yet we know in faith, if we've done any kind of personal and serious reflection through the years, that we are being transformed as a church and are being led to the destiny which we originally surmised and sought after.

If young persons come to inquire about our way, it is sufficient that the pilgrims say that our journey is difficult and the way often unknown, but that we move to God. Our direction is purposeful though sometimes uncertain. For a people used to instant definition of the most profound mysteries, this new stance is obviously painful. It is God who has summoned us to this journey away from the place we used to live in our minds and hearts. With confidence, we invite those who choose to come along with us on the pilgrimage. We promise no material advantage, but we do promise meaning and inclusion in the community of faith. We promise a new liberty and the freedom of the sons and the daughters of God. Think of the impact this attitude about church could make on the Catholic mother and father entering the inevitable struggle with the teenager who has decided not to go to church. We have such a long way to go to understand what the religious journey is all about. We badly need to comprehend that our difficult life-journeys and our Catholicism are not irreconcilable opposites but in fact one and the same pilgrimage after God.

The symbol of pilgrim offers great possibilities for identifying ourselves as church. The contemplative recognizes the significance immediately, but the radical insecurity of it boggles our minds and halts our footsteps. Let's get to a motel that has hot showers; never mind the endless, struggling journey. Religion should be neat, clean and manageable. Yet the symbol lives deep within us and explains the way we are presently feeling about ourselves. It also gives us direction. There is, after all, much we know about pilgrims that helps us feel that our present journey is not worthless and futile. As we think about the symbol, it certainly does seem to capture the reality of who we are. Once named pilgrim, we can be confident that our sometimes straying footsteps are warranted; they move within the design of the provident God.

There are further questions we may deliberate if, in fact, this symbol communicates our reality. Are the hierarchy those marching at the head of the ranks in the role of leader or are they struggling pilgrims among other struggling pilgrims? Is their task one of running alongside the moving body, prodding persons to stay in the line? How are we to explain the various roles in church if we identify ourselves as a pilgrim people? The contemplative can be easy with the task of working all of this out. It is, after all, a part of the pilgrimage. No one has promised us a rose garden neatly mapped out. It is for the pilgrims together, including our leadership, to study the signs of the times which indicate the presence and the direction of the Spirit.

We should substitute for the words "uniform and predictable" the words "diverse and different" when

177

we ponder the reality of church. We are nationally at ease with pluralism and diversity in a multi-ethnic, multi-religious land, yet we expected uniformity in our ecclesial lives. Some immense changes have been asked of us whereas our former experience of church had been one of stability. Almost without warning we were forced to encounter the chaotic and the formless even within the institution we thought impregnable to social change. We could have remained in the fortress if it had hidden itself on a backroad away from the mainstream of human history. We were not a frightened people, but the wounds inflicted by the reform movements of the 16th century had caused us to ward off any further blows of misfortune and splintering.

We are finally comprehending that it is not a question of whether we like the changes or not, as if they are somehow arbitrary and subject to whims. The work of restoration of age-old and proper meanings is gradual and painful. We are learning that in confronting the formless and the chaotic, it must be we who, with personal, creative maturity, shape and fashion, in the power of the Spirit, who we are to become. We give direction to our pilgrimage as we move to God. Infantile dependencies have to be discarded. No one can tell us what we ought to do in all situations. There is no one whose permission we must obtain to carry out the major decisions of our lives. No one except ourselves can ever take ultimate responsibility for our lives. At the end of our days, we must face the Lord with the sum of choices we have made during our lifetime. We made decisions, right and wrong, for which we take sole responsibility. All of us pilgrims are co-responsible for the kingdom of God. The blind must see, the deaf hear, the lame walk, and the poor have the Gospel preached to them. This is our common Christian mission.

The contemplative is not frightened by such seeming formlessness and unpredictability. It is a factor in all aspects of human existence including the ecclesial. The contemplative learned to forego the childhood wish that all life be fair and that all occurrences be planned and well-ordered. Disintegration is a painful but ever-present reality. What we do with the chaotic is what makes the difference. For Catholics the move from a great sense of order within the enclave has given way to an overwhelming need for establishing order. We must direct our progress without setting in concrete a road which pilgrim feet must tread for all time. Pilgrims can't be confined to the one and only yellow brick road. They must have sufficient liberty to move in whatever perilous direction the Lord seems to be calling them even when they suspect they may be listening to a drum that gives only an indistinct beat. The true pilgrim has some native instinct that the Lord God will beat the foolishness out of us on the journey, a disquieting yet enlivening adventure.

The central mystery of our faith is the death and resurrection of Jesus and the identification of these occurrences in our own lives, both in reality and in sacrament. The mystery of passage offers us yet another symbol by which to recognize ourselves as a particular church people. We see that our lives follow a creation-destruction pattern. We die and we rise. We gain some things; we lose others. Ups and downs form the content of each day. We find this to be true not only for ourselves, but also for our families, parishes, religious communities, civic and national groups. Sometimes we are able to recognize these transforming moments, but most of the time we are uncertain how to define each confusing and unsettling experience.

Jesus Christ gave a particular significance to the fact of death and rebirth. He died and was raised up and the passage became the possibility for the transformation of all humankind. Unless the grain of wheat die, it remains alone. Others would follow after him and define their lives in this salvific context. He had called the powers of evil and absurdity by name and in parabolic action had redeemed us from them.

Once raised from some shattering human experience, we wish not to die again. Revolutionaries presume that theirs will be the last mortal struggle, but revolutions come and go. We die, and we die again. Most of us have lived long enough to see that the irrational and the absurd in human existence continues despite our best efforts at eradication. We have also learned, however, that it is the absurd that purifies us of our illusions. Each time we are forced up against the absurd, we are compelled to deal with it, to change, grow and shift gears, or to capitulate before it, give up and die. The problematic is that the absurd is so absurd. If only it made some sense, and if only it weren't stupid and irrational, we could deal with it with some dispatch, cast it off with aplomb and march on once again as victors. But the truth about the absurd is that it is absurd. It tears us down, causes us to be humiliated and embarrassed, makes us hate and suspect ourselves, and question over and over again whether we have any right at all to hold up our heads as humans, let alone as Catholics and followers of Jesus. As a contemplative moves through the dyings, we gain new levels of integration. We focus on real problems and situations and we abandon the fantasies we've woven concerning how things shall go.

The symbol of passage is thus another way by which we understand ourselves as church. We are a people who die many times and who are transformed into the image of Jesus by God's power of deliverance. Although faith recognizes the mystery of passage, it does not make it any easier to cope with dying times. This symbol clarifies a particular identity for us, but it is often one we wish we could forget. We do not like to die.

When society receives non-threatening and tamed religions politely, church people can allow themselves to become weak and insignificant in order to be accepted. We make no waves and no one is challenged by our words or actions. The symbol of wilderness and diaspora implies that we may have to leave ecclesial and social ghettos. As we become a people moving through utterly unfamiliar surroundings and as we find ourselves as scattered pockets of believers here and there, we will know ourselves not as a church swept along by social custom but, in fact, a people who have made personal decisions for faith. Sometimes we are called to leave all things, even what we have named holy and sacred inside and outside of ourselves. We are summoned by God to move again and again into the wilderness. In faith we sense that this mysterious and lonely setting is somehow the tenting place of Yahweh, yet so much of it seems arid waste. We wish for leaders capable of reconnoitering, and sometimes God, in a tender and gracious fidelity, provides a few. Most of the time paths have to be beaten and are not there to be discovered. The meaning of the wilderness is the work of the multiple decisions

and choices we must make along the way. So often the
march seems futile and we long for the old securities
which the wilderness does not contain. Quail and man-
na appear occasionally but they remain suspect because,
like our spiritual ancestors, we ask: "What is it?" We
can't even fathom the nature of the blessings of the
wilderness. Why diaspora and disestablishment when
we have worked so hard in this country for establishment? Why must we continually step away from any security base we establish either individually or corporately in order once again to plunge into the unknown?

We want to find God in joys and prosperity. It somehow smacks of a personal failure fraught with guilt if
God is present only by means of absence. If in the
wrong turns and in the bitter days, God seems gone
from this stormy and ill-defined journey, we somehow
very quickly blame ourselves. Repeatedly we confine
the unlimited and eternal Godhead to our puny notions
of how it must be that God will act. The church needs to
pray for conversion; we must pray to be turned around
and given the grace to know that being flipped over on
our backs on the shore like some washed-up sea crab is
a true religious experience for us. It is one which will
push us into the arms of God more quickly than all the
splendid rational insights we might conceive or all the
wonderful feelings of devotion that surge over us in moments of religious highs. God acts in our despair. God
acts when we're turned upside down. God's power acts
in our abysmal weakness. God leads the church in a
continuous exodus.

The contemplative knows the experience of being dis-
established. It is a part of every day. The scattering
experience of diaspora is not a new occurrence and so in

the wilderness the contemplative is the one in the community who can offer some plausibility structures to the others. Some people depend upon things being made plausible for them, but the contemplative creates the structures which make sense of the wasteland. The poet, Don Lee wrote in "Changes" that although a black person wants all kinds of things changed—the law, the institutions, and "whitey"—the major thing to be changed about any of us is our mind. Contemplatives have had to change. The Lord has never let us meander in our own footprints for very long. One remembers the saying of Cardinal Newman which underscores this wisdom: "To live is to change. And to be perfect is to have changed often." The contemplative has welcomed the process of frequent change as the only means to integration.

One of the areas of change for the church is the radical departure from presupposing our reality to be defined by Western Europe. Catholicism is meeting sons and daughters who have no native European roots. Their ways of articulating the nature of God, their understanding of faith-community, their music and sacramental celebrations call us to examine once again the text of Galatians: neither slave nor free, neither male nor female, neither Jew nor gentile. One adds: neither European, Roman, American, Canadian, African, Asian nor any other structure by which we may choose to divide peoples. We are all one in Christ. Jesus is manifested to us from all corners of the earth. There are many more comings of Jesus than we had presumed. Usually we have confined his comings to only those styles which we approve. The contemplative, as a person of heightened awareness and sensitivity does not thunder past the serendipity of God. Here is something valuable, someone not explicitly sought. The moment or person is unexpected, yet the eyes of faith and wisdom behold the advent of God. The contemplative sets no barriers on time and place, east or west, oriental or occidental, joy or pain. God comes! Let the church rejoice!

These symbols of church—pilgrim, passage, wilderness, and diaspora—are clarion calls to faith. In the enclave faith was somehow simpler because everybody looked and acted the same way as ourselves. On the pilgrimage and in the wilderness, in the face of impossible darkness and inevitable mis-communication, a great deal of sheer faith is imperative. We have been called to shift paradigms and to give up comfortable shelters in order to search out the directions to which the Spirit is pointing.

The path demands an extraordinary form of asceticism for the church. We are to relinquish everything and enter a dark night in which the roads of our journey are uncertain and unclear. We are to trust that this dark night will eventually be creative and fruitful for us. We have a choice either to trust the Lord enough to move faithfully into the wilderness of unfamiliar territory and into a possible diaspora situation or else to surround ourselves with the scattered bricks of the enclave trying vainly to reconstruct our former dwelling. Brief campsites for decision-making are necessary, but we can't lose too much time dallying along the way. The contemplative is ready for the exodus; all of life has been marked by an exodus from anything to which we might have clung. With an exquisitely balanced sense of realism the contemplative knows the meaning of the daily journeys of death and resurrection. We have been pilgrims most of our lives.

It is by means of all these symbols that the contemplative presently defines the nature of church. The symbols tell us who we are and clarify our present situation. They enable us to make decisions and to trust that God continues to be present to the church. If the religious experience of many church members verifies these symbols, it is yet another indication that the contemplative life is not something so far away from us after all. The Spirit is summoning the church to holiness. We will answer with a readiness for the journey or we will pretend we hear nothing in the winds of change but disorder and disorientation. The judgment of the truth of our pilgrimage will be based on the quality of our mission to the afflicted and the urgency with which we proclaim God's reign during the years ahead.

The church as institution has not always approved the contemplative; in fact, the history of contemplatives has been beset by a good amount of criticism of them as a gnostic elite who claimed insights denied to others. Obviously their religious experiences had to be tested against the bulwark of orthodoxy. Genuine contemplatives, however, were persons of immense loyalties to the church. They were the first to mistrust their visions and they historically bent their wills to those of lacklustre popes, bishops, and theologians. We read their biographies marveling at how they managed to remain within a structure which oppressed, yet which posthumously blessed and canonized them. Those who, by God's grace, had integrated faith and life apparently offered some nameless challenge to those who were dependent on outside forces for their identity. Whatever the evil forces are that stalk our world, they seem compelled to put contemplatives to the test. Surely, their motives are impure; surely there is some peculiarity about their dogged clinging to a vision that is amorphous, untutored, and perhaps even heretical. These contemplatives had to be checked out and called upon to answer for their views. Walking on the water was out. Rational analysis alone could be trusted.

The contemplative has a particular understanding of church institution and its authority structures, because there is a direct relationship between one's dependence on authority and one's own religious experience. If our experience that God has in fact acted in our lives through persons and events is minimal, the more totally dependent we will be on authority for directing our spiritual steps. If we feel certain that God has been present to the details of our days, then it is with some conviction that we chart the course of our immediate journey. If we have never learned to recognize or to trust God's deeds in our personal histories, we will need an outside resource which will interpret our times and tell us how to celebrate liturgy correctly, live morally, or even seek after the face of God in a particular manner.

Contemplatives have come to understand the nature of church institution and thus of authority differently as a direct result of the renewal of biblical studies in our recent past. Jesus gave authority to his disciples against evil and for healing. Jesus said the greatest were the least. His own redemptive work bore the character of servant leadership. The Christian scripture mentions the gift of administration within the Body of Christ; it is one of the gifts used for the growth of the community.

Scholarly study of the Bible was authorized as late in our history as 1943 by Pope Pius XII with the encyclical *Divino Afflante Spiritu.* From that time to the present, Catholics have had available the finest in biblical interpretation. We had been strictly warned against individual interpretation of the scriptures since the Council of Trent. What happened, of course, was that not only individual interpretation but any individual reading or scriptural prayer was foreign to most Catholics. The scriptures were opened only in liturgy as we listened to the explanations of the pericopes chosen for Sunday worship. Since 1943, the power of the word has been brought to us in parish lectures, in numerous books and in sermons preached by those trained by excellent scholars. Our children are receiving adequate training in the sacred writings of our faith community. The scriptures form the bedrock of our present piety instead of the collection of spiritual books, however valuable, of the last few centuries. If discrepancies arise between the word of Jesus and the actions of church people, the contradiction forces the contemplative to an examination of conscience as well as to becoming a voice by which the irrevocable power of the two-edged sword of the word confronts the tawdriness and the shabbiness of a church which can stray far from our original call and mission.

The contemplative knows that those who possess the gift of authority hold a sacred trust. Authority is defined from a scriptural model of service for the kingdom rather than from a secular model of domination over others. Any misuse of the sacred renders great pain to one sensitized to the gospel. The implications about the nature of authority derived from the scriptures have offered us a conceptualization of authority different from that prevalent in the church for hundreds of years.

The contemplative person whose portrait we are drawing is not one who is a deceiver of anyone, least of all of ourselves. The loyalty of the contemplative to persons in authority is genuine within that framework that presumes loyalty to include calling oneself, the friend, the family, and the church community to a renewal of faith if we are to be a leaven in our world. At certain times loyal dissent within the church is a service to a people who continually need to clear vision and praxis from the accretions with which time and custom overlay even the most precious traditions. The contemplative searches conscience repeatedly as to whether or not the message of Jesus is at the heart of the proclamation or whether vested interests have crept in to obscure the word. The true contemplative lives on the razor's edge of a healthy self-doubt and is thus able to scrutinize ecclesial purposes with a clear eye. Teresa of Avila attributes ambivalences about themselves and a serious and consistent self-scrutiny even to those persons who have been brought by God's grace into the seventh and highest castle of interiority. God is not doubted but our integrity and authenticity come under an attentive surveillance most all the time.

The contemplative who confronts the church is to be distinguished from the perpetually and pathologically angry person who vents childhood rages against present situations and whose rhetoric may be the coming of the kingdom but whose primary motivating force is obviously self-aggrandizement. Not so the contemplative. There is in this person the vague fear and the overwhelming sense of an unwillingness to die, yet a rather certain sense that radical discipleship will cost even more than this. Anger is a powerfully motivating force and the contemplative is not without it, but this anger is born of wisdom and channeled against real injustices wherever they are found.

The sadness that we face, of course, is that injustice is not just in some far-off country where drawn guns are a part of the main street scenery. Injustice is to be found right within the church where vocations cannot be followed because ministries and executive leadership are denied persons by reason of sex; financial data is unavailable when in fact the money belongs corporately to the faith community; property is bought and sold without any discussion in the councils of the community. A corporation sole, whether of husband, wife, bishop or teen-ager seems somehow to indicate everything that is not church as the gospel outlines church and as Vatican II further defined us. Insofar as church authority views its task as juridical, managerial, fiscal, or triumphal rather than as a gift given for the reign of God, serious conflict will ensue between irreconciliable models of authority.

John Paul II teaches the importance of dissent to the vitality of a community in his book, *The Acting Person*. The dissent of loyal daughters and sons within the church itself needs to be seen as vital to its growth and to its fidelity to the word of Jesus. As serious Christians we ask to investigate all the implications which the scriptural understanding of authority carries. We patiently try to clarify the relationship between fidelity to the church as institution and dissent against the grave difficulties which the institution occasions. Is the authority structure in the church shaped by the gospel?

Are decisions about faith, life and mission shared responsibilities? Is the presence of the Spirit evident as directions are chosen? Does the community assemble for prayer and discernment as it charts its course?

The Greek root words which form our word hierarchy convey the sense of the sacred. Authority in the church pertains to the mystery of God's providential designs for humankind. That the kingdom come with its evident healings is intrinsically connected to the nature of authority. The gift of authority which Jesus gave over the forces of evil is focused in particular men and women. Theirs is the sacred trust to see that the community of the faithful remains true to the word of God. The reminders by Jesus against worldly power are many; no church leader can afford to be blind to the encroachments of secularism with its futile lures. It is nothing but pathetic to find religious superiors, bishops, or pastors who view themselves, however subtly, as managers of a corporation.

The contemplative's experience of the divine is of great significance to the way a contemplative views authority figures. As we recognize God present within all the details of our lives, God is not set out over against history but rather within it acting to save. If God is not a distant Lord and Master ordering the earth, it can be posited, as does Gregory Baum, that one's experience of authority as pyramidal as well as of one's experience of a world order as unchangeable, is radically altered. Authority is not focused in some distant Lord and Master but in one of the pilgrims among other pilgrims who yet possesses the gift of sacred authority in order that the kingdom come. This should be something of a relief to those in administration at any given time. Their teaching, governing and sanctifying office is not carried on in a vacuum, but rather is faithfully accomplished right within the community and in co-responsible dialogue with the faithful who also have received a mandate for the kingdom from the Lord Jesus. If, among the faithful, there are those who, because of ill health of mind or body, need someone to make their life decisions, one may assess this action as charity or healing; it certainly is not connected with the dialectic of authority and obedience.

Co-responsibility for the kingdom does not remove from leadership the lonely burden which genuine leadership always involves, but it does insist on a collaborative model for authority in the church. It is obvious to the contemplative that the winds of change are blowing cleanly and clearly around the question of authority. Former models are recognized as insufficient simply because too many of us are only repelled by that which is clearly out of focus with the gospel. It is unfortunate that the power structures of Roman Catholicism are crumbling not from the forces of evil, but from ineffectual leadership both clerical and lay. There is a particular sadness about this circumstance because the ministry of authority for the good of the kingdom is left untended as the juridical is spelled out over and over again to empty pews. Monied Catholics with connections to ecclesiastical power can continue to support the crumbling structures, but the call of Jesus for change has been heard in the land and heard in the hearts of too many of us. It is a call which we know must be taken seriously. The contemplative senses that if we do not move away from the niceties of a socially acceptable religion, the Lord will find other ways and other peoples who will answer the call to discipleship.

The contemplative weeps in the night over the many problems of institutionalized discipleship. The church is a great and holy body of people, yet we have never failed to admit our sinfulness, as well. When we confront our sin, and that of our brothers and sisters, we weep for the pain we cause one another, but more, we weep for the gospel witness which is obscured and for the ministry which is thwarted. We must call ourselves and our leaders to that vision of church which seems directional and Spirit-given. We have not completed nor shall we ever complete the task of renewal until the church as people and as institution is eternally in harmony with the word of God. The integration begins now; it is the work of us earthlings into whose weakness the Lord has entrusted the power for the kingdom.

CHAPTER NINE

The Experience of Love

LOVE is what God is. We are to become what God is. We are to become love. This is the simplest way one can put into words the goal and summit of our lives. The contemplative stands in awe before the mystery of love because we well know that unless love is what we become, all of our living shall have had no meaning and no particular direction or reason.

At almost each wedding we attend, we hear the reading from Paul to the Corinthians: "Love is patient; love is kind. Love is never jealous; it does not put on airs. It is never rude, self-seeking, nor prone to anger. Love does not brood over injuries nor does it ever fail. In the end there will be three things that will last—faith, hope and love. The greatest of these is love." We watch yet another bride and groom seem utterly confident of what love will require of them. If asked, they can admit that there will be some hard times, but the powerful feelings they presently know for each other will certainly carry them past the shoals upon which other marriages have broken up.

This same scripture is interpreted by many of us as a spiritual task to be accomplished. "I must become a more loving person. I will try to be more patient and kind." We nag at ourselves interminably as we contrast our behavior with the passage. Only as experience

forms into wisdom does the contemplative know that
the words are in fact a description of God. God is patient and kind. God is not jealous, does not brood over
injuries, nor does God ever fail. To presume that by
taking thought and disciplining ourselves we can carry
off the task of loving is preposterous and the repeated
attempts and failures which we have witnessed in ourselves and others should corroborate this idea. What is
supposed to happen in the course of our lives is that by
God's grace we are to become what God is. Recall again
the prayer from our liturgy: "Jesus became a partaker
of our humanity so that we might become partakers of
his divinity." We are to become love. As this grace
commences in us, we will know interiorly a patience and
a kindness that is not the result of our own determina-
tion for good behavior but rather the power of God
forcing us beyond our own capabilities.

What we usually term love might better be called
"like." Like is a feeling while love is a lifetime project.
It is only over many years spent relating to others that
love is tested and authenticated. It becomes the truth of
our commitment, not merely its pledge. The Roman
philosopher Plotinus uses an allegory in the *Enneads* to
describe humanity's penchant for grasping quickly at
what is close at hand instead of investigating that which
is more remote yet which is indeed the heart of the matter. The anecdote helps us detect our usual superficial
and facile approach to the topic of love.

Plotinus speaks of foolish persons who watched the
triumphal procession of a great king. There were wonders and marvels which delighted and captivated their
minds. But being foolish persons, some went home
before they ever saw the face of the king. They thought

the initial pomp and splendor were everything. The king came at the end of the parade. They did not wait. They were satisfied with the panoply which had gone before and never realized that they had missed the central point of the whole parade.

The story can tell us that what we glibly say of love probably falls far short of its reality. We take the fireworks and display of the early stages of meeting for what must be a long term and gradually developing enterprise. Only after some time can we claim to know the meaning of love at all, although there are glimpses all along the way if our awareness is sharp and acute.

What is love? Love is what God is. St. John knew this. He insisted upon the truth of the declaration and spoke very forcibly to the Christian community who proclaimed it, that they would therefore have to live lives that concretely showed their love for one another. The ramifications of the assertion that God is love are very definite and not in the least abstract. If we say we love God, yet act without love toward a sister or brother, then what we have called love for God is a lie. It is a cheap and pathetic religious illusion with which we try to deceive ourselves and others. We are liars not because we might tell an occasional lie, but because we live piously in some distorted universe comprised of our own conscious or unconscious projections from a fundamentally disordered religiosity.

The people of the Old Testament recognized that God acted toward them with loving kindness and fidelity. They did not conceptualize this love of God essentially or eminently. They perceived it manifest in the loving deeds which encompassed their lives and which, in their faith, they knew as God's presence. Enemies were conquered, lands were discovered, and life went on in the community through failure and success. Their God was tenting among them with love. Yahweh's fidelity was like a straight road stretching limitlessly and directly toward the horizon.

For the Christian believer, the loving kindness and fidelity of God became flesh in the person of Jesus Christ. We could see with mortal eyes what God looked like. God looked just like us. The divine grace and truth radically immanent in Jesus was shown in an extraordinary and godly love which culminated in death on a cross. Jesus preached and taught the God whom he knew. He never changed the message he felt compelled to preach. So great was his love for us and so great his love for God, that Jesus defied even the religious persons of his time to tell us in very real terms what love looked like. If need be, love might cost one's life being freely laid down for the friend or enemy.

After the extraordinary deed of the cross, authentic love would always have a sacrificial aspect to it. No warm fuzzies here—rather a love which endured the consequences of a charge of blasphemy and ultimately death. Jesus' love was controverted because it had upset the apple carts of normalcy and propriety. It was a love far beyond what was demanded or necessary. Surely the man exaggerated. Yahweh could hardly be concerned for the riff-raff of society who hadn't bothered with temple duties for a very long time. Love, after all, had to fit into the religious schemes of the times. Love could not act outside the established customs and admit a Samaritan or a prodigal. Love certainly did not need to seek out the lepers, the crippled, the beggars, the sinners or the other categories of undesirables. "If you love those who love you, what is the good? I say to you love one another. Do good to those who hate you. Love your enemies.''

The mandates to love which are a radical part of the Christian dispensation are not rules we have to obey if we want to remain in the club. They are not commands which we are supposed to force ourselves to carry out. We must change our minds and comprehend that God is love, that this love is incarnate in Jesus, and further, that this love is incarnate in us just as we are; therefore, these mandates are intrinsic to a love which is participative in divinity. We are rooted and grounded in love, says Paul. The love we offer another is connected with the very life of God. It is a love that, whether we know it or feel it, is an extension of God into historical terms. The love which God is, is incarnate in us because of the mystery of uncreated grace. Theologically this grace has been defined as identical with the life of the Godhead. It is gift and grace bestowed on us.

The only problem we have with all this wonderful and inspiring language is that love is incarnate in us just the way we are. If, like the Peanuts cartoon suggests, "I am an open-faced crab sandwich," then God's love is incarnate precisely in our crab sandwich selves. We have psychological wounds that take a lifetime to be healed. Foolishness tracks our steps within our cultivated weaknesses and stubborn resistances. Scars caused by old betrayals and rejections have not healed. We have particular cultural and ethnic backgrounds which have narrowed our capabilities for warmth and openness. There are specific stages of human maturation and we can love only with the present mechanisms for loving that we possess. We may be emotionally embroiled in a love affair which has blinded us to the real nature of love. These are the subjective dispositions in which love becomes incarnate once again.

It is the work of years to allow love to heal and forgive, to open and expand, to change and reshape our clay. The work of becoming love, of becoming what God is, is accomplished only in a whole lifetime. It is upon completing this task of love that we will be judged. The potentials for patience, for kindness, for never failing in love and for moving beyond jealousies are all within us waiting to be freed into act. The initial step of freeing that love is to love ourselves enough to be able to reach out with truth toward the other.

If we think about love this way, it changes our image of how to go about it. Instead of viewing it as something that we have to try hard to do or as a task to work at despite our shortcomings, our efforts are a process of gradually discovering the love in which we are rooted and grounded. Love can lie dormant inside us, fruitless and unproductive. Another is then unable to be touched by our love or we to respond to theirs. If we let them, certain people will come along who will enable us to peel off, in one way or another, the layers of hurts and psychic wounds which impede the dynamism of love. When we let life happen to us—with its various persons and destinies which are in fact God's doing—it will change us and make us new. We will be able to become love.

When we speak of loving God, most of us conceptualize this action only in terms of relationship. "I am the I and God is the Other who loves me and who is to be loved in return." Sometimes our efforts at loving God seem only so many futile gestures toward an invisible friend who is supposedly walking beside us and guarding our footsteps. There is, however, another way for us to conceive the idea of our love of God and God's love for us than in the category of relationship.

The epistle to the Ephesians points to the way of identification. This was spelled out as the contemplative's experience of God. This person finds it increasingly impossible to deal with God in terms of an Other. If love must be conceived in terms of relationship, we are compelled to something that has become experientially impossible. The contemplative's experience of the divine seems always so peculiarly different. The rhetoric of many people suggests their experience of God as one of relationship. They seem to live their lives before a Thou always somewhere and somehow present in their consciousness. The contemplative goes through life feeling like some misbegotten atheist because absence seems to character God's manner of being with us. How can one love what is absent? The mysterious answer seems to be that for the contemplative, love has become a matter of identification. The sense of the other is gone, but the sense of becoming love confronts us daily with presence and with surprise. What on earth does this mean?

The finality of any love should be a profound unity and oneness of being, yet in human terms, oneness is never entirely achieved. By grace we are brought into identification with God. We can become what God is. With a great reverence and a holy fear we are gradually filled with all the fullness of God about which the author of Ephesians writes.

How can such a phenomenon occur without some bizarre interpretation being placed on it? All the egoists of the world may announce themselves as contemplative and thus ward off any criticism against rude and paranoid behavior. Certainly unless some fruits of gentleness, tolerance, and receptivity are evident in one's life, any talk of a contemplative lifestyle is only so much jumping on the bandwagon of some new jargon. The true contemplative knows only that in this matter of loving, life and time are very ordinary. There is no great feeling of devotion or conflagration of love. There are the ordinary daily choices and decisions which show in deeds the love that is claimed in word. Identification so articulated blesses our ordinary experiences. In the faith and in the worldview of the contemplative, God has chosen to act in the ordinary. The proof of this statement for us is the mystery of the incarnation. There is no invisible friend to love. There is only this day with its tasks, and these persons to welcome and by whom to be welcomed. All of it is somehow in God. All of it is God. All of it is love. All of it has to do with our becoming love.

The Spirit of God has gathered the world into the mystery of the trinitarian Godhead and this is demonstrated every time that an act of concrete love is performed in the world. Love has to do with getting up in the morning, with working patiently and perseveringly, with dealing with all kinds of people, the happy and the querulous. It has to do with letters to be typed, floors to be scrubbed, jobs to be done, babies to be cared for, buses, trains, civil rights, aid to the handicapped, the women's movement—the list is endless. We are engaged in what *The Cloud of Unknowing* refers to as the contemplative work of love.

Yet we are reluctant to find love so ordinary. Surely there must be something in it that is sublime and that might sweep us off our feet. There is, but it is always very ordinary. We love the big parade, but perhaps the king who comes at the end of this one comes poor, lowly and seated on an ass. We would like Jesus to turn out to be somebody extraordinary, a person of some external splendor who causes in us a burst of ecstatic outcry. Jesus is all of this, but only as we come to know that he sits down to eat a meal side by side with us each day. The king's name is Emmanuel. God with us. Who sat next to us at lunch today? Only faith can answer. Pagan eyes demand something other than the typewriter, the files, the crumbs, the kitchen floor or the neighbors.

Science fiction thrillers of enormous scenic proportions have given us some extraordinary shots of spaceships breaking beyond the speed of light. The work of contemplative love is nicely captured by this image. With more or less difficulty we try to act lovingly, to do loving deeds, to offer what we understand to be God's love to others. But it is when we are seized and grasped by God beyond our own efforts at loving that we become love.

How does this occur? All through our lives we face people and situations that force us to die to our own notions about things and shift into different gears to deal with reality. In these instances we can choose to die forever with our sparse ideas and plans or we can choose a life that offers some different options for behavior. When, with God's love drawing us, we continue to choose life rather than death, we become love. Pain and struggle surround us, but they do not become our reality. Instead we are chastened and purified by life's fires. We pass by the barriers of our own acts of loving to engage in the continuing extension of God's love and merciful designs among humankind. Faith tells us this is so. Hope allows us to trust that it is so. Love occurs in us. Through life's challenges and demands we can become warm and loving, or we can become hard, embittered, cantankerous and selfish. The choice is ours.

The word which qualifies our becoming love is spontaneity. Our acts of love are not studied. We move quickly and sensitively to the gesture of love. *The Cloud* speaks of the fruit of a contemplative life as an increased sensitivity; that is, we become more surely and accurately in touch with the other. We are able to absorb the pain which comes out from another person, as Bernanos so strikingly says. The healing influence of the sensitive person is like a swift and deft touch to the pain-filled area which heals and cures because it is true and unerring. We have been brusquely insensitive or felt we were treated insensitively by another. The quality of sensitivity suggests that one is able to walk in another's moccasins skillfully and exactly. It does not take a sensitive person a year to figure out what someone is trying to say or to comprehend their non-verbal communications. If we are becoming more finely honed and refined by the fires of our own life processes, then, commensurately, we can become more keenly aware of another. We can reach out with exquisite tenderness into another's life, into another's pain and into another's delight to rejoice and be merry with them.

In the *Analects,* the story is told of Confucius that when the barn burned, the master merely asked if anyone were hurt. He did not lament the destruction of the building or the monies that were lost. He was sensitive to the human situation. We betray our lack of sensitivity when someone comes to tell us of an earache and we interrupt to tell them of an earache we once had. While we're still narrating our long story, the person walks away in frustration because we were totally unavailable to their pain and discomfort. We try to explain the difficulty we're having getting a paper ready for a class we're taking and the entire neighborhood seems drawn to tell us about every term paper they've written since third grade and how difficult it was for them to complete it. Someone stumbles over a piece of furniture in a friend's living room and the hostess nervously alleges that she had just vacuumed the room, a remark plainly irrelevant to the accident. All these incidents betray the person who looks out at life from the egotistical narrowness of a self-centered universe. We cannot reach out because we are hopelessly entangled in ourselves. All of life is funneled and sifted through our perspective. We are really never in touch with anybody else. We are utterly, primarily, and preferentially concerned with ourselves. The sensitive human being reaches out quickly and quietly to the exact meaning of a situation with an exquisite sense of assessing the moment for what it holds. The insensitive person tramples the present moment crushing its every possibility for revelation.

Current psychology and indeed common sense informs us that we must love ourselves, gain self-esteem and believe in our own worth. But authentic love must move beyond this initial and necessary phase to the place where one's life can be given for the other. We find ourselves very far away from the summons to a sacrificial love. The neurotic manifestations of those who drone on about their lonely goodness has sickened us to the notion. In addition, we live in times which advertise self-assertion. No one will walk all over us. We demand what's coming to us. We gripe and complain against everything and everybody in order to absolve ourselves from any real involvement which might produce a change in some difficult situation. Our energies and our time commitments are seldom where our mouths are. When we love, however, the shallowness of the preceding is evident. Love pushes us beyond our bigoted viewpoints into a kind of divine expansiveness.

An author of a book on Zen describes the enlightenment experience as engendering a heightened awareness of all reality. Prior to enlightenment, he had walked around oblivious to most people, situations and even to the natural environment. After the experience, he saw the field flowers and did not crush them. He was present to his life. He was awake and alive to the moment. It is obviously only this sensitive person who can know what it means to become love.

Becoming love means becoming conceptless in loving. We don't plan how we're going to love someone; we simply love them in deeds and with genuine concern. Mere words and great emotional embroilment can be part of the expression of love but can never substitute for its presence. When we mistake emotional embroilment for love, we will have to go through many sad moments until we are really able to love. There is nothing wrong with being emotionally embroiled with someone; many of us are embroiled many times. All we need to know is that this chemical attraction or whatever it is, is not really what love is.

Teresa of Avila was emotionally involved with someone during practically all of her first twenty years in the cloister. She loved passionately and completely. She needed to learn and did, that freedom must become a part of our loving. It is a dual freedom. Our lives can never be totally tangled in with another's and we must always allow the other the freedom to be. Ultimately no human being can be a home for us; nor are we ever ultimately a home for someone else. Yet love demands that we open ourselves continually to be home and hearth to the stranger, the alien, and above all, the possible friend and the loved one.

Like Teresa, it is exhilarating to live life with passion. It is always so much more interesting to meet someone who lives passionately than someone who presents us with the handshake of a limp fish and a demeanor which is not much different. If a hostess were to invite five dull and five interesting people to a dinner, at which table would we be sitting? To be a person of passion will mean that our emotions, our feelings and our reasons are nicely tied together and our potentialities are functioning at their maximum. We are not half our possible selves.

Living life passionately has to do with trusting life and people and gradually moving out of the confines of our mental cocoons to make some changes in our customs. So frequently we are afraid to open our lives to another, because they may take advantage of us, betray us or hurt us in some way. Shakespeare was right when he wrote that if you could find a good friend you should bind the person to your soul with hoops of steel. It takes time, effort and patience to try to be a friend, yet there is no way for us to become love except through loving. Birds, cats, and dogs will not do. We must love real live human beings who can talk back to us and who can never live up to our hopes and dreams for them as we cannot ever live up to theirs. We need to be able at least to conceive in our minds the possibilities of other relationships besides those of the family and the immediate community. It is not enough to love those who love you. There must be other loves in our lives beside the few we have captive within our immediate circles.

How do we begin? We know only our family with its various extensions and perhaps the couple next door. A simple way might be to make a list of people we like. Then write next to their names anything we've done to encourage a friendship or acquaintance with them. Usually we haven't much to write because we've rehearsed the same script for so long: "I haven't time." "They probably wouldn't want me to bother them." "I'm too tired." We also exhibit some tangles in our heads when we include on our lists the mayor, the bishop, a well-known writer or singer, and we are dismayed when they cannot respond to our overtures because of their already heavily committed schedules. Obviously there must be some possibility for initial meeting and mutual response in order to start a relationship.

Aquinas' designations of relationships as useful, delightful or worthwhile show us how varied are our connections with one another. The best relationships are the ones which include all three components. Friendship in marriage and outside of it is a project to be worked at over long years until, gradually, we perceive the beauty and strength of the many faceted relationships that are at once useful, delightful and worthwhile to us in the finest of senses.

Friendship is different from a counseling relationship or a "do-for" relationship, and we must learn to make this distinction lest, naively, we presume friendship where it is not. Friendship is a two-way street that assumes that we have become a friend to ourselves. The friendless people of the world are not persons whom others have rejected but persons who have rejected themselves. Much has to get straightened out in our closedness, so that love can enter. Divine love pounds against our closed doors ceaselessly by means of the lady down the street or some other circumstance that confronts us and causes us to make some new moves. We can choose to hide and close our options. We can refuse to become love.

We need to provide enough space and time in our heads and in our calendars to let relationships happen. Mostly we're too nervous about it and we play our cards close to our chests. We feel we have a lot to lose if another person really got to know us. Perhaps they will not like what they find.

In relating to others, we learn about ourselves. We learn how small and how great we are, and how we think our ways of doing things are the only ways. If we can allow the other to be and to challenge us and we inversely to challenge them, we can become love. Love is the hardest thing that a human being has to do and for many it has become so impossible and so hurtful that they have decided to forget about it, to exist on very superficial levels, and to reside in the corners of their minds sufficient to themselves amid their own books and games. We can then never become love. They can never be what God is: patient, kind, not jealous, never-failing, not prone to anger and all the rest. They will end their days wizened, selfish, and puny of vision because the only power strong enough to break all the bonds that tangle their hearts and minds was sloughed off because they were afraid.

Fortunately if we are at all open to it, the power of

God's love operating in multiple human circumstances breaks through the walls within which we have been hiding. That love can cause us to grow emotionally from being 8, 10, 12 years old and from operating out of childish and immature patterns. God wants us to become love. We will never reach the fullness of our human potential until the work of love is wrought in us. We can kid ourselves and others, we can hide away for years, but eventually the task is laid before us and we must choose to love or choose to die.

Our loves can gradually move beyond natural likes and become universal. We will be able to reach out to those who do not love us in return. We can care for the unlovable, the brash, the paranoid, the utterly bothersome. The sacrifice demanded in these relationships is immense. We must have a keen sense of the difference between being a doormat and being a saint. Only by the power of God can we swallow harsh replies or continue to be receptive when our instinct is to lash out and take revenge. Self-canonized martyrs will presume they know all that this means. Unfortunately, love has nothing to do with pathological needs for rejection. There is always such a fine line between madness and holiness. Regretably, much of the rhetoric of the two sounds the same.

As God's love is revealed at the center of our reality and as we are progressively enabled to love ourselves, we become love as we deal with another. It seems to us that this is a requisite to coming before the face of God after physical death. We cannot meet God unless we have become what God is. We cannot become love until we have loved regular, ordinary human people who are right around us in all the normal ups and downs of trying to understand who and what another is. Once again, religious experience is so ordinary. Loving is not something off in the clouds; it has nothing to do with how we feel. It has everything to do with what we do, with what we are, and with what we are enabled to become by the power of God.

It is possible to see all of this happening in us. Love is the measure of the authenticity of our Christian life and certainly of our prayer lives. Those who say they pray and their lives give no evidence whatsoever of love are charlatans at worst and very sick individuals at best. The entirety of the Christian dispensation is based on love. "Did you give the cup of water? Did you reach out in mercy? Did you visit prisons and console the afflicted?" Nothing else really matters. Though we may deliver our bodies to be burned, though we may speak with the tongues of angels, unless we have love, we have nothing.

Love is the hardest thing we will ever have to do. It takes years to understand what it's all about. A mother of some teenagers continually says to them: "I'm not just clacking my teeth." In respect to the mandates to love, Jesus was never just clacking his teeth. Either we become this love or we have missed the entire meaning of Christianity. Frankly, it is very scary. The fruits of the Holy Spirit will become evident as the process of God's love takes its course through our days. There is so much in us that prevents love's happening. We must seek the counseling, the spiritual direction or the advice that can bring us past the place where we're stalled. We cannot really die well unless we have learned to live. There will have to be some kind of time outside of time in which we can achieve loving humanly if we do not achieve it while we live in this physical body. Perhaps this is what the concept of purgatory means. We must pray to love enough. We must pray on each birthday to love enough so that we are ready to die. Loving is so very hard, because it is so daily and so mundane. It requires our lives given for others. No melodrama here—no exaggeration—no clacking of teeth. Love is what we are to become.

Our attempts will often be futile and exaggerated, immature and stumbling, but the one who makes attempts at loving is far healthier than the one who has opted to remain alone, hidden and silent, in some sad little recess of the heart or mind.

In the extraordinary mystery of Jesus Christ is the example of someone who loved, totally and completely. There was no turning back, no change of purpose, no revenge, and no smallness of vision. Jesus said yes. His decision to continue the course he had begun caused his death by murder, yet, with divine omnipotence, the whole event was transformed into salvation and meaning.

This is just crazy! Everyone does not have to do this. It's enough to live a quiet, decent life and not bug the others in our family or neighborhood. No, it isn't enough. We were made for God; we were made for love. We were made to become love. All of this takes place in the very ordinary actions of each day. No matter that we falter and that we sin, the task of love is constantly before us. It is what we must demand of life. It is a task gigantic enough to compel our entire being into the enterprise. It is an enterprise in and with God.

Love is an act that surpasses justice. Aquinas was right when he suggested this. Certainly if we've offered a phony charity that did not rest on the secure foundation of justice, our charity was hollow and false. Justice gives what is due, but charity gives what is undeserved, what is not due, and what is godly. Charity extends into eternity.

Ignatius concludes his *Spiritual Exercises* with the superb meditation on love. He has led the retreatant through pondering the entirety of personal as well as all of salvation history. Out of immense and overflowing gratitude, the retreatant can sing and pray: "Take, Lord, receive all I am and all I'll ever have. You have given all to me. I return it. Give me only your love and your grace. That's enough for me." This prayer proceeds from the heart of one who knows what love is.

The followers and disciples of Jesus are the crazy ones of the world who must attempt to love sacrificially. As Zorba said, one needs a little madness to break the ropes that bind and so be free. To try to become love asks so much of us. After all, one has to be realistic. "Let those who can hear, hear." There is no point in getting into an argument about this question of loving. It is what Christianity is all about—take it or leave it. Christianity is not about ritual and moral living except insofar as these two express the love that causes both of them. We must at least pray for the grace to be able to pray to become love.

It is so very hard. The ones who think they are loving are probably not. We have to be wary of our own deceits in this regard. We can go around smiling through our teeth like villains in plays but this is not love. We can ask to do things for people only to learn, as the years pass, that much of our strained generosity issues from pent-up rage. We can give and give to another and find that we have done every scrap of this out of our own needs. All of these failings on our part are normal and human. We are not to browbeat ourselves. It is only that we must be very realistic. So much of what we have paraded off as love of others is nothing but ego projection. Pray God for truth in this matter. Pray to be broken out of the straightjackets of warped ways of trying to love. But above all, continue to make any and all attempts at loving, because it is only through doing this, that we can proceed on the path of becoming love at all.

Ultimately this is what the Christian celebration of Eucharist is all about. All of this? Yes. We come to do what Jesus did. We come to say we've tried to love. We come to say we've done it badly much of the time, but we renew ourselves and our intentions for love over and over again. The words at the consecration—"Do this in remembrance of me"—are broader in meaning than a command to get together every once in a while for thirty minutes to do this ritual. What we are to do in remembrance of Jesus is live the life that Jesus lives, to die many times, and to be transformed into love.

The Christian cannot escape the consequence that someone might despise us enough to seek our ruin. We ought not use the word cross to name our aches and pains, our ups and downs, or all the self-rejections to which we so desperately cling. We must admit that the cross is what happened to Jesus because of the way he lived. In our own experience the cross might be a very real possibility if we follow the road of sacrificial love. Nothing phony here, nothing very easy. Though many may try to deceive, we know the genuine article of love when we find it. Any other talk or gesture is palaver and pretense. The contemplative knows that love is what God is.

CHAPTER TEN

The Experience of the Path

FOR so many years any words exhorting people to lead a holy life seemed to exclude most of us because of the extensive spiritual exercises that were prescribed. Monks and nuns had the leisure to pursue holiness whereas the laity were to be working in the world; we were to christianize it and render justice in the public forums. We could relish the fact that behind the scenes somewhere there were people who were praying, who had sold everything they had, who had abandoned husband, wife and lands for the gospel and who had not turned away sad when Jesus delivered the message about how best to become disciples.

Any true path to holiness seemingly had to contain within it the time-tested procedures of the monastery. After all, these had worked well as structures within which many had been aided in their journey to God. The monastic model of spirituality had given a rhetoric and many specific sets of directions for going about a spiritual life. Definite times of silence and of prayer, the deliberate reduction of multiple sense stimuli, submission of one's will to the spiritual leader, recitation of the Liturgy of the Hours, hard work, the renunciation of exclusive relationships and the abandonment of any fruitfulness to one's sexuality were the components of the model. One must seek God emptied and alone—an extremely valuable truth indeed, but one which needs individualized application for each one who undertakes the path to holiness. Whatever holiness was all about, it apparently had nothing to do with those who had to file income tax forms, who had to commute to work, who had to shovel snow and figure out where the money would come from to get the kids through school. We were the householders; monks and nuns were the ones with the special call and the leisure necessary to pursue the divine.

We have needed to rethink what holiness looks like. A good definition to pursue is that holiness is an exquisite balance in us between an utter love which demands complete responsibility for our lives and an utter freedom which demands that nothing at all entangle our hearts. This state of being begins to be evident in the truly holy woman or man. We have frequently mistaken some outward signs of poor posture, ill-fitting clothing and personal peculiarities, coupled with much time spent in church as evidences of whatever it is we named holiness. But when God graces our world with the truly holy individual, we have met a person in whose life love and freedom are precisely balanced and functioning. It is a terrible beauty indeed. These persons do not come from any particular walk of life; they wear no distinctive costume. They are fat and thin, tall and short, smart and not-so-smart, but God's power has brought them into being loving and free simultaneously in daily practical instances.

Quite a number of years ago, Catholics began to be encouraged to participate in the ministry of the hierarchy. We were called lay apostles. Vatican II took up this earlier summons and urged parishes to call upon their lay members for many of the ministries that shape parish life. "Step aside for the laity," was the cry of the religious professionals. "The laity have come of age."

My personal notion is that it is the era of disciples. Either all of us, whatever group we're in, are going to determine what following Jesus is all about and get on with it, or we should fold up our evangelization kits and hibernate for the long winter of our demise. Thankfully, we have felt the spring thaw of the Spirit's warming the frozen categories of cleric, lay, religious, or episcopal, and the Spirit's broadening our concepts about who could do what in proclaiming the reign of God and in healing the afflicted. Hand in hand, across color, sex, role, and credal lines, we are hearing a new summons and are joining together to explore and follow a path to holiness for the mission of the kingdom. What does it mean to be a follower of Jesus in our world? Can one seek holiness while remaining a part of the daily work force? "Come and follow me" surely was not issued to some elite corps but to those who heard and could find in their hearts a profound response to the summons to discipleship.

A model of a holy life or the outline of a spirituality suitable for who we are today is difficult to come by. Former models urged some time each day in prayer and meditation and, on a daily or weekly basis, some serious spritual reading. Frequent celebration of the sacraments was to dot our days. Some prayer in common with others, a time apart for retreat, and places where we could hide from families and friends to be quiet and to pray and reflect—all were essential and unalterable components of a holy life. Indeed the prayer of perspective is necessary, yet though each spiritual exercise named is important and time tested, still, for most of us, the prescribed path is impossible. Time each day? We can hardly keep body and soul together and get our own and the families' shoes tied before running out the door. We long for reflection periods and feel guilty when we watch football. If we didn't watch all this TV perhaps we could spend more quiet time, perhaps even walk or run or get in some exercise. Guilt usually doesn't exert enough power for any change, however, and frankly we so badly need the recuperation time which watching a game brings. This is not to canonize television and the isolation of watching it to the detriment of relationship, but to admit that the pace of our society demands the solitude that many find watching wretchedly valueless programs.

The components of a contemporary spiritual life have to fit into an era characterized by multiple involvements outside the immediate family and community circles which place rigid demands on our time. There is, however, a path to holiness for busy people that does not remove us from the daily but grounds us more wittily in it as we are enabled to shed the escapist daydreams of what we have wished a holy life to be.

This contemporary spirituality has a traditional name: contemplation. A spirituality is a means of establishing serious contact with the divine. All the spiritual practices enumerated offer that contact but most of the methods are outside what is practical for our lives except in some limited ways. Contemplation is an apostolic spirituality and, as I have outlined it, it can form the spiritual undergirding for the demands our present life and times put upon us. It is a life of holiness and a path to God which suits a people on pilgrimage. Contemplation, because it has carried with it a history of presence to life, suits women or men whose lives are sometimes frantic and filled with incessant claims. The contemplative life is indeed accessible to us because the Spirit of God is drawing us to it.

Many theological currents have entered the discussion that has allowed us to consider and articulate our path to holiness as one of contemplation. The classics of mysticism have come into our hands through the transmitters of wisdom in the community. We have found the contemplatives and mystics eminently practical persons who exhibit human greatness concomitant with human stupidity. Through the excellent work of our scripture professors and research scholars, we have witnessed the renewal in biblical studies and have come to recognize, as never before, that God has acted in human history in human terms. Our teachers taught us well that the crowning point of the divine intention was the incarnation, and that the implications of this divine act have something to do with our daily lives. That God has become a man blesses human experience forever as the locus of the divine activity. We err if we yearn for some pie-in-the-sky religious dispensation. The theology of incarnation teaches that if we are going to see the face of God, we will have to look upon the face of the man, Jesus. Because of Jesus and his revelation of God's nature to us, we gradually realized that the further extension of incarnation means that when we look for God, we will have to find God in the faces of the human beings in our world. Even current psychology has warned us that if we carve images of deities and jump up and down in pogo-stick adoration before them while trouncing upon the hearts and feelings of our neighbors, our whirling and leaping is only so much confused motion, a rattling of beads, some sound and fury but no substance.

God became what we are in Jesus Christ. Current christologies have laid stress on the humanity of Jesus, not to the omission of divinity nor the denial of it, but to insist that only by looking squarely at the human and only by comprehending deeply what it reveals are we able to surmise the divine. Any other path to God misrepresents the incarnation. God intends that we find the divine within ourselves and within our world of people and daily happenings. Anything else is falsification and religious illusion.

None of this is to deny God nor to divinize humanity except in the way that Jesus divinized it. There is God but it is a God who tents with us while we explore the unknown terrain of our days. This God acts but always and only in the ordinary episodes of each day. Only faith beholds that what is occurring today is redemptively significant. Without faith, we do not see the grace of the immediate moment. Salvation is all around us and within us, as people grow and change, and the church is renewed through the power of God's presence in historical events.

The secularization theologies, which some claim stem directly from Aquinas, blessed our earth and named us responsible for it. Aquinas had spoken of our having dominion over the universe, a reality which included ourselves and our environment. We were to care for God's creation, guard it, and deliver it into eternity. This sacred stewardship for our world was entrusted to us by the fact of our creation. When we destroy what

God has made, we go against the order intrinsic to creation.

For long years we viewed this responsibility within the context of a particular worldview which, in our rhetoric, was that of an enclosed unit. Within the circle there was a pyramidal structuring of roles by which we all knew our place and could explain quickly and exactly who and what we were under God. Jesus had left a sacramental system which kept us in touch with the divine and we went about our daily tasks with a fairly peaceful and contented sense of our identity. Holiness had to do with living well and piously our role in life.

Suddenly, in the course of our lifetimes, we find ourselves viewing reality very differently. The circular and enclosed world of the church was blown open and we saw history stretching ahead of us for our ordering, our creating and our saving—all because this was God's design. Many psycho-sociological, scientific and historical forces had converged to shatter our construct. Overnight, we were a people on the march. We were unable to feel encompassed by a divine plan which had God in heaven and all right with the world. History extended forever ahead of us; process and flux now characterized what had previously been the equilibrium of eternal stability. We would have no permanence again except that which would be established through our creative maturity aided by the power of God's grace.

If this were our task and if we needed a holiness of life to accomplish it, we felt at first that we were going to have to carry the entire monastery on our backs as we marched along on our pilgrimage. We were encumbered with the only methods of seeking a spiritual life we knew. Even if we decided to carry the monastery in our hearts—a not unfelicitous idea—nonetheless, there was too much of what a monastic spirituality correctly or incorrectly connoted that did not serve pilgrims.

What had to happen of course and what did happen is that the contemplatives among our number began to notify us that the way to proceed would be to interiorize the programs of holiness—a process always at the heart of all spiritual programs anyway. We are finally to realize that we must become prayer and that we are to be persons totally immersed in faith so that we think and act differently each day because we believe. It has been hard for us to do this, and nearly impossible for some of us, because we had become so used to computing holiness and structuring its achievement. So much time had to be put in at prayer, so many Masses heard or rosaries said, so many visits to church or chapel to find God, and so many times away from people in order to be alone for godly things—all these had to be the content of our spiritual exercising. These actions could be tabulated and recorded, and with each one checked off, we could breath a sigh of satisfied accomplishment.

We find an enlightening example of the meaning of interiorization in the East Indians who for centuries have cited four stages which lead to a highpoint of human integration. These four prove useful to our explanation of the nature of interiority, a task incumbent upon every maturing human person.

The first stage of human developing is that of the celibate student. Here one initiates the move to adult awareness. The young person seeks wisdom and accepts teacher, instruction, and a life of discipline, all vitally necessary for beginners. The householder, as the succeeding stage is designated, embraces responsibility for home and world, a normal progression from novice who is cared for, to adept who must accept caring for others. As genuine seekers advance to greater maturity, they seek to dwell in the forest away from the responsibilities of householder. Forest-dwellers leave the established patterns of their lives and seek the silent wisdom of the forest accompanied by their families. The final and holiest stage is comprised of those who discover in themselves the readiness to renounce and abandon everything—family and possessions—and depart as homeless and exiled wanderers to seek the Ultimate.

Each of these stages can be read as actual, physical moves to geographical places or they can be interpreted as interior journeys. We must note immediately that to define these stages symbolically is not to underestimate the value of external, bodily peregrinations. We are, however, all too sadly familiar with the phenomenon of religious fakes who speak of, or look like they have renounced everything but who have renounced nothing, least of all themselves. Thus whether one journeys in material or internal space, what is imperative about stages or processes is that they be authentic acts of interiorization.

The celibate student times for us are those years in which we build structures of meaning for ourselves with the help of various mentors. We know that if we choose to pursue certain goals, we have to avoid the entanglements that take up too much of the time we need to grapple with who we are and what we're trying to become. Whether we marry or not, we move from this beginning stage to that of householder. We assume responsibilities for ourselves and for the various communities with which our lives are intertwined. The first impact of responsibility captures our imaginations and challenges our creative energies; we move to our undertakings with an initial kind of delighted commitment. Later the weight of multiple burdens takes its toll of our dedications. This stage bears continual examination so that it never becomes a mindless plodding from one day to the next.

Generally, the time comes for us householders when we acknowledge an inner ability to close off many of the avenues through which we have been traveling. We no longer need to surround ourselves with comforts and securities. We intuitively apprehend that we are in sight of some final wisdom about life and we know an innate capability to go after it. Without hardly noticing it, the householder becomes the forest-dweller; we do not relinquish anything of our lives except what is foolish, time-wasting, and useless. The broad expanse of forest-wisdom unfolds indeterminably before us with its intimations of richness and its promise of immortality. We move into it with a glad eagerness to be away from the tedious concerns with which we formerly spent our days. In this stage, relationships become richer and are not abandoned.

But beyond the forest lies the prescience of complete and utter renunciation. Now we must set aside everything we think we are, everything we think we can do, and every person who has become a part of our lives. We move to the freedom, liberty of spirit, and utter detachment which command our leaving everything we have and are, to seek justice and peace away from the complexities of motivations obscuring why we do anything we set out to do. The spectre of renunciation frightens us, but somehow, instinctively, we know it to be an irrevocable demand placed upon our lives. We will have to renounce even the results of our labors ultimately. We can retain nothing for ourselves. The purification unmistakable in this language terrifies us. We do not like nor seek refining fires, but it is the Lord who leads, compels and graces us to this final stage. Through it we are enabled to prepare for the consummate union with the divine. The Face we have sought will at last be right before us and we shall be so surprised because we shall just have eaten lunch across the table from that same face only very recently.

We do not name our various stages of maturation by these Indian titles, nor are we often consciously aware of our progressions nor overly concerned about them. But the insights about our humanity's psychic development are universally true and offer us a clarifying wisdom which can guide our steps. The four stages are the work of a lifetime. However, they can occur cyclically, that is, we may move through all four stages many times because of different life junctures. When we have to begin again, however, we will know a new depth. We recognize these stages of our developing though we may trace them somewhat differently from the ancients of India. None of them necessarily means moving geographically or leaving anyone or anything except interiorly.

Sometimes we get locked into one stage and fear the move into the next. This is a most unfortunate human circumstance because we are then brought to a stalemate. We die bogged down there without ever experiencing that life, love, and joy which await us in the next and more requiring stage. We are reluctant to let go of the little portions of life and love of which we can now be absolutely certain and assured.

The interiorization process just delineated lies at the heart of the explanation of what the Spirit is causing in our times. Our path to holiness is presently distinguished by the interiorization of faith rather than by the assertion that to be in the church is in itself an evidence of salvation. This is a major shift in the paradigm of what it means to be a Catholic. Our former conception that we were somehow better or closer to God and truer to God's revelation than all others has given way to the perception that we are all called to radical discipleship. We have judged a need to re-evangelize the structures of the church as well as to preach the gospel to any who have not heard it nor seen its evidence in the lives of Christians. If we are responsive and alert to the divine advents, our daily experiences become the locus of the divine activity in our world. We do not seek God in a distant far off heaven but right within human history where God has chosen to act. God seems to be summoning us to this interiority. Ours is a life in which, at least eventually, everything fits together. Though we know the inevitability of our fits and starts, still the gradual integration of all opposites and polarities has begun. Integrity will never occur in us if we fight and claw to manage our lives and everyone else's. But if we can live with an eagerness, with a sense of possibility, adventure, and joy, we will know that providence has in fact undergirded our every day.

The path we walk has certain identifiable components. Since the spirituality useful within a monastery is not totally helpful to the pilgrim journey, we are ready, I believe, to summarize the factors which comprise a spirituality for our times. We have seen its designation to be contemplation. With all the qualifications spelled out previously, the components are these:

1) *God experienced within life* . . .

2) *Jesus Christ's death and life re-presented in our own* . . .

3) *An urgency for the coming of the kingdom* . . .

4) *A renunciation stemming directly from our commitment to proclamation and healing* . . .

5) *Our prayer as a contemplative presence in the world* . . .

6) *An overwhelming awakening to the meaning of power in weakness* . . .

7) *A growing desire to hear a call to racial discipleship* . . .

8) *An interiorization of faith* . . .

9) *An inability to separate life and praxis* . . .

10) *A growing demand that justice be done and that we be involved in its happening* . . .

11) *An agonizing search for a simpler lifestyle* . . .

If Alice in Wonderland could hear about contemplation, she would repeat her famous complaint: "That's an awful lot for one word to mean." Yes, it means a lot because the reality of the contemplative life permeates the totality of our existence. There is no thought or act that is not stamped with its seal. God, transcendent and immanent, encompasses our days. No part of them, even the disintegrating forces, is outside of the dispositions of Providence.

Teresa of Avila specified that the persons who had reached the seventh castle of interiority understand what the rest of us hold in faith. She struggles to express this clearly as she says she doesn't mean any kind of imaginative visions or sight. It is unmistakable that the persons so described are the contemplatives of the world. Faith has pervaded life. They are what they do. For these persons, religious experience has nothing to do with the bizarre or the religiously costumed. We still rebel against the ordinariness of contemplation. The contemplative knows, however, that the only thing that ever really matters is not ebullient feelings of devotion or scintillating spiritual insights, but concrete acts of love, justice and mercy. The contemplative has learned the wisdom that what is important is not the times in which we live but how we live in these times.

Living life contemplatively changes everything and it changes nothing. The ordinary is as it is, but the paradox has clarified the path. The contemplatives will be surprised at the end of their days to learn they had assessed experience correctly. Experience is the locus of the divine activity.